Y0-BVN-775

John A. Dixon is a Research Associate at the Environment and Policy Institute (EAPI) of the East–West Center, Honolulu. He is an economist and is the leader of the Institute's applied economic analysis activities. Dr Dixon has extensive experience in Asia working with both national governments and international agencies.

Richard A. Carpenter is also a Research Associate at EAPI. He is a chemist whose principal interest is environmental assessment.

Louise A. Fallon and **Paul B. Sherman** are both Research Fellows at EAPI. Dr Fallon is an economist with a background in biology and a strong interest in resource management. Mr Sherman is also an economist and specializes in natural resource and environmental issues.

Supachit Manopimoke is an East–West Center grantee from Thailand. She is a PhD candidate in agricultural and resource economics.

Economic Analysis of the Environmental Impacts of Development Projects

John A. Dixon, Richard A. Carpenter,
Louise A. Fallon, Paul B. Sherman and
Supachit Manopimoke

EARTHSCAN PUBLICATIONS LIMITED · LONDON *in association
with* THE ASIAN DEVELOPMENT BANK · MANILA

First edition published 1986 by
The Asian Development Bank
This edition published 1988 by
Earthscan Publications Limited,
3 Endsleigh Street, London WC1H 0DD

British Library Cataloguing in Publication Data

Economic analysis of the environmental impacts
    of development.
    1. Environment. Effects of economic
development
    I. Dixon, John A. (John Alexander), 1946–
304.28

ISBN   1-85383-015-1

Earthscan Publications Limited is an editorially independent
but wholly owned subsidiary of the International Institute for
Environment and Development (IIED).

Typeset by Florencetype Limited, Kewstoke, Avon
Printed and bound in Great Britain by Richard Clay

Contents

Preface   vii
Authors' Foreword   ix

1 Development projects, their impact on the environment and
   the role of economic analysis   1

2 The use of environmental assessment for analyzing impacts
   of development projects on natural resources
   and the environment   6

3 Economic measurement of impacts on the environment – theoretical
   basis and practical applications   19

4 Generally applicable techniques   35

5 Potentially applicable techniques   50

6 Additional methods of valuing environmental impacts   64

7 The limits to economic measurement of environmental impacts   77

   Appendix: Case Studies   86

References   126
Index   130

Preface

The past decade has witnessed a growing realization that economic development and environmental awareness are not contradictory goals. The interrelated nature of economic growth, natural resource use, and environmental protection is encompassed by the phrase "sustainable development", which describes those activities that promote the long-term, sensible use of the natural resource base. The Asian Development Bank (ADB), an international finance institution with headquarters in Manila, Philippines, has been actively involved in the effort to promote development which is economically and environmentally sustainable.

The ADB's Environment Unit has supported the development of guidelines and procedures to ensure that environmental aspects of development are given ample consideration. Realizing the importance of translating environmental concerns into monetary terms to achieve this aim, the Environment Unit has cooperated with ADB's Economics Office to commission the writing of Economics Staff Paper No. 31, *Economic Analysis of Environmental Impacts of Development Projects* by John Dixon and others of the East-West Center in Honolulu, Hawaii. This report was prepared for use by Bank staff. It has been well received and distributed to a number of Bank member countries and other international development agencies and finance institutions for training and as a reference document.

The report focuses on what can be done given varying degrees of data, manpower and financial resources. The valuation techniques presented are grouped according to their direct applicability to the types of environmental and resource effects commonly found in development projects. Obviously, this brief volume cannot cover all valuation approaches in detail. References to the published literature direct the interested reader to fuller discussions of different techniques. The case studies illustrate the use of selected techniques and approaches.

As a result of growing interest in this topic – the economic analysis of environmental and natural resource effects of major development projects – the ADB is supporting the commercial publication of this report in the present form so that it can reach a wider international audience. To suit publication needs the authors have revised the original manuscript and have included additional material, partly in response to feedback received in various training courses and seminars in the two years since it was originally published. References to recent literature have also been added.

The Asian Development Bank is pleased to make this important and timely material available and looks forward to continuing involvement in this area.

Asian Development Bank
Manila, Philippines

Authors' Foreword

During the past several years, the East-West Center's Environment and Policy Institute, under the initial leadership of Maynard M. Hufschmidt, has undertaken the applied benefit-cost analysis project which has led to the publication of two books (Hufschmidt *et al.*, 1983 and Dixon and Hufschmidt, 1986) and other supporting materials.

In 1985 we were commissioned by the Asian Development Bank to prepare a report based on our earlier experience of this work. The authors wish to thank the ADB for its support in the preparation of the initial version of this book. Special thanks go to Burnham O. Campbell, Chief Economist, J. Keith Johnson, Economist, and Colin P. Rees, Environment Specialist, and numerous other Bank officers who gave useful comments on the draft, suggested appropriate examples of Bank projects, and provided access to Bank documents. This report was published in 1986.

Between publication as an ADB Economic Staff Paper and this commercial publication, we have received valuable help and advice from many sources. At the Asian Development Bank, Bindu N. Lohani, Head, Environment Unit, has provided a continuation of the support offered by his predecessor, Colin P. Rees. Mr George V. Liu of the Information Office and Mr E. Suzuki of the Office of the General Counsel have been supportive and helpful in the complex process of bringing this work to publication.

Numerous professional colleagues and development specialists have read and commented on the initial report, including Professor Jack Knetsch of Simon Fraser University, Vancouver, Canada, and Ms Regina Gregory of the Environment and Policy Institute, East–West Center. We welcome comments on this book and would like to hear from others who are working on the challenging topic of applying economic analysis to the environmental and resource impacts of development projects.

1 *Development projects, their impact on the environment and the role of economic analysis*

Economic development, the ultimate goal of which is to improve human welfare, is crucially dependent on the environment and natural resources to provide the goods and services which directly and indirectly generate socioeconomic benefits. At the same time, however, economic development is often accompanied by significant adverse impacts on the environment. This has led to the belief that economic growth and environmental conservation are mutually exclusive. Many people still feel that some deterioration in environmental quality is a necessary and justifiable cost of economic growth, and also that the management of natural resources for sustainable use is a luxury which poor developing nations can ill afford. However, a growing body of opinion has gradually emerged which recognizes that degradation of the environment and misuse of natural resources will result in real losses in the long term and, furthermore, will undermine the basic objective of development – the sustainable improvement of human welfare.

Governments in developing countries are becoming increasingly aware that environmental and natural resource degradation endangers the potential for long-term development. As a result, they are becoming more receptive to the implementation of measures which ensure that development projects take both the environment and natural resources into account.

Many countries have experienced instances where the degradation of their natural resource base has resulted in the impairment of long-term growth. One common instance is that of fisheries, both inland and marine, damaged by water polluted by domestic and industrial effluents. In some areas this damage has reduced the traditional primary source of protein. Another example is the deforestation of upland regions produced by both shifting agriculture and excessive timber extraction for fuel and wood products. This has led to the disruption of the hydrological cycle of major watersheds and has caused erosion, siltation of rivers and reservoirs, and increases in both the incidence and severity of flooding. The result of all this has been a significant reduction in the productivity of many forests, agricultural lands, and fisheries. It has also decreased the returns from major investments in hydroelectric power and irrigation schemes.

Most people in developing countries work on the land and are directly dependent on natural resources for their food, shelter, and employment. Their welfare in both the short and the long term is inextricably tied to the productivity of natural systems. Thus the socioeconomic effects of degraded environments often hit the poor hardest. It is clear that successful economic development depends on the rational use of environmental resources and on minimizing, as far as possible, the adverse impacts of development projects. This can be done by improving project selection, planning, design and implementation.

Both bilateral and multilateral institutions devoted to funding development projects and programs see their role as promoting the most efficient use of available resources within the context of the socioeconomic priorities of the individual developing countries. Economic analyses of alternative development projects must therefore assess both the direct and indirect benefits and costs of proposed actions. Such analyses require a broader perspective – one that includes the whole range of benefits and costs involved in the proposed activity.

Most lending institutions feel that the direct economic costs of a project are relatively easy to quantify, except where significant externalities such as environmental impacts are involved. Even in these cases, they realize that the costs of such effects should be quantified as far as possible, but the difficulties involved in this process have prevented this quantification; hence environmental effects have often been described and evaluated only in qualitative terms. The real question, therefore, is: How can the environmental impacts of development projects be identified, quantified, and valued?

There are two major elements in assessing environmental impacts: first, they have to be identified and measured; second, ways must be found to place monetary values on these impacts so that they can be included in the formal analyses of projects. Only when a monetary value cannot be given to a particular environmental impact should it be dealt with qualitatively within the analyses.

Both components are reviewed in this book, and suggestions are given as to how economic measurement of environmental impacts generated by development projects may be undertaken. The approach and techniques presented are based on work done over the past five years by researchers at the East-West Center Environment and Policy Institute (EAPI) in Hawaii, with collaborators in the United States and Asia. The techniques themselves have been developed by economists around the world; the EAPI contribution has been to synthesize existing information and provide a practical application of the techniques to handle environmental quality effects of development projects.[1]

This book focuses on the better analysis of *projects* and their environmental or resource impacts. We do not deny the major importance of macro-level government policies on the patterns of resource use. Such policies as pricing of fertilizer, pesticides, and water have major impacts, both good and bad, on resource use and the environment. Similarly, trade policies, foreign exchange rates, the use of taxes or subsidies all have far-reaching impacts. Nevertheless, the development, analysis, and funding of discrete projects is a major form of economic development in all parts of the world. These projects are the focus of this work.

The Analytical Sequence

Projects are frequently identified and developed in a process known as the project cycle. Figure 1 illustrates the main components of the project cycle used by the Asian Development Bank, but similar patterns are used by the World Bank and other major regional development banks (Rees, 1983). There are numerous places within the project cycle where environmental and resource concerns may be injected. It is crucial, however, that these concerns are taken into account early in the cycle, during the design stage. Only in this way can alternatives be considered before too much time and

---

[1] The work has resulted in the publication of a book: M.M. Hufschmidt *et al.*, *Environment, Natural Systems, and Development: An Economic Valuation Guide* (Johns Hopkins University Press, 1983), referred to in this volume as the *Guide*. A case-study workbook illustrating the techniques has also been published: J.A. Dixon and M.M. Hufschmidt (eds), *Economic Valuation Techniques for the Environment* (Johns Hopkins University Press, 1986).

3

FIGURE 1:
Project Cycle

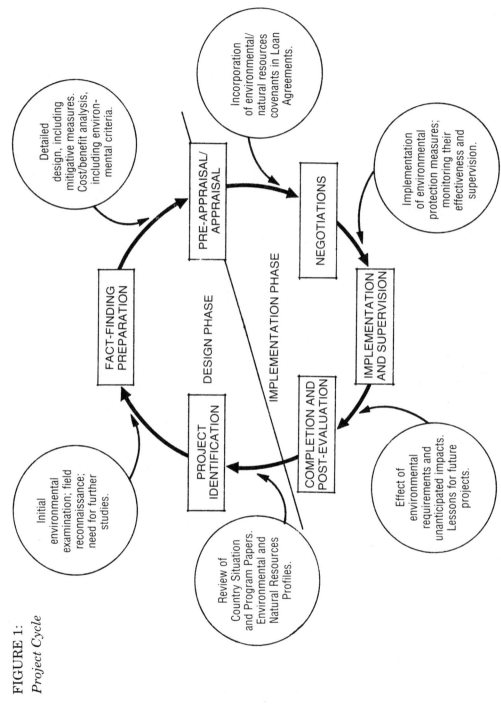

Source: Asian Development Bank (1986), *Environmental Planning and Management*

4

effort have been invested in one concept. The project designers must work in a multidisciplinary team to design projects that consider a variety of goods and services – economic, social, environmental – at the same time.

The purpose of this book is to demonstrate the use of this new analytical approach and to provide a range of techniques with which to determine the monetary values for the impacts of projects on the environment. The use of environmental assessment procedures, valuable at the early stages of project identification, are discussed in Chapter 2. The remaining chapters of the book deal with attributing monetary values to the environmental impacts. The basic theoretical assumptions underlying our proposed approach to valuation are outlined in Chapter 3. The techniques themselves are presented in Chapters 4, 5, and 6; Chapter 4 focuses on techniques that are generally applicable to project analysis, while Chapters 5 and 6 concentrate on techniques which are more difficult to apply and whose use in project analysis has therefore been limited. Chapter 5 covers potentially applicable techniques that rely on the existence of surrogate markets or the use of cost-analysis approaches. Chapter 6 presents the use of survey-based techniques and introduces macroeconomic, mathematical models. The limitations of the economic measurement of environmental impacts are discussed in Chapter 7.

In the interests of brevity we summarize each technique, discuss its applicability and illustrate its use. Several case studies, which illustrate complete economic analyses as well as the use of individual techniques, are presented in the Appendix.

2 *The use of environmental assessment for analyzing the impacts of development projects on natural resources and the environment*

Environmental and natural resource degradation can be the result of existing conditions as well as of projects designed to promote economic development. For example, extensive rural poverty and intense population pressure can exert stress on productive natural systems: the degradation of range and pasture lands as a consequence of overgrazing; the loss of productive soil as a consequence of inappropriate agricultural practices and poorly designed irrigation schemes; the loss of productive forests as a consequence of shifting agriculture and fuelwood collection are all examples of such pressures. Urban areas are equally affected as the influx of people from the countryside overtaxes facilities and gives rise to polluted water and air, congestion and increased incidence of disease. To the extent that these problems are the result of inadequate development, some of their solutions may lie in well-planned economic growth. On the other hand, economic growth itself frequently results in environmental and resource degradation.

These unwanted consequences of development need not, however, occur, since the technical and managerial means of preventing and controlling them exist. Many current problems have arisen from overexploitation of natural resources or poor planning and design of development projects, coupled with inadequate assessment of potential impacts. It is rarely a simple choice between development and the environment; rather, it is generally a question of incorporating sensible measures for environmental protection into the earliest stages of development projects. Without systematic

6

analysis, however, potential problems will not be recognized early enough to allow for the examination of alternative approaches within the project.[1]

Environmental assessment involves identifying, quantifying, predicting and evaluating the impacts of various development activities on natural resources and the environment. It complements the conventional package of engineering, socioeconomic and financial analyses and provides a practical aid to project analysts. The methods of assessment are systematic and allow the recognition of appropriate opportunities for development as well as warning when the degradation of sustainable production capabilities seems likely.[2]

Undertaking the Analysis

As far as possible, systematic attention should be given to environmental aspects in all phases of the development project, and this should begin at the initial stages of project formulation and preparation. Only then can costly errors in conception and design be avoided.

Natural systems are holistic and interconnected.[3] Consequently it is essential from the very beginning of the planning process to determine carefully which natural systems will be affected. A "scoping process" may be used to set appropriate boundaries – the geographical limits, time horizon, and the range of issues, actions, interrelationships, alternatives and impacts that need to be considered. When appropriate, natural boundaries should be used: for example, the watershed is often a good planning and management unit.

Three criteria for identifying significant impacts on the environment were suggested in the World Conservation Strategy.[4] The first concerns the

[1] A comprehensive survey of the consequences of economic development for natural systems is given in *Natural Systems for Development: What Planners Need to Know*, ed. R.A. Carpenter (Macmillan, 1983).
[2] Sustainable development is a strategy to achieve immediate economic gains while maintaining indefinitely the productive potential of the renewable resource base.
[3] A natural system, or ecosystem, is a dynamic arrangement of plants and animals with their surroundings of soil, air, water, nutrients and energy. For example, lakes, rainforests, mangrove forests, and grasslands are ecosystems; so are rice paddies, oil palm plantations, fish ponds, pastures and home gardens. As the latter are all modified by human beings, they are called "managed systems" and are often less complex in comparison to the diversity of undisturbed environments.
[4] International Union for the Conservation of Nature and Natural Resources (IUCN), 1980: *World Conservation Strategy* (Geneva).

length of time and geographic area over which the effect will be felt. This criterion would include an assessment of the numbers of people affected, how much of a particular resource would be degraded, eliminated or – depending on what action is taken – conserved. The second criterion is that of *urgency*. It is important to establish just how quickly a natural system might deteriorate and how much time is available for its stabilization or enhancement. Finally, it is important to assess the *degree of irreversible damage* to communities of plants and animals, to life-support systems, and to soil and water.

There are several other criteria which are relevant to this identification process. One important consideration is the nature of the effects on the environment including such issues as health, agricultural productivity and changes in micro-climate. The assessment should also take into account the cumulative and synergistic effects of the various components of the project as well as considering each component separately.[5] The effects of individual projects or of their component parts may be small, but cumulatively they may become considerable. Further, the effects of two or more projects in the same region may be far greater than could be predicted by the sum of their individual effects.

The next step is to quantify, as far as possible, all the important biophysical and socioeconomic changes that are likely to result from the project. These might include, for example, the intrusion of salinity into groundwater; price changes induced by new energy policies, programs and projects; the impacts of disposal of industrial effluents; deforestation as a result of building new highways, and so on. Not all of these effects may be quantifiable; when such effects cannot be quantified they should at least be noted qualitatively.

In order to quantify these impacts, it is first necessary to measure environmental quality parameters before the project has begun. The quality of the air and water supplies, the fertility of the soil, the nature and quality of the habitat must all be measured. These data on baseline conditions and trends make possible the assessment of changes produced specifically by the

---

[5] In this context the Asian Development Bank has sponsored the development of a series of regional master plans which examine the ecosystemic linkages among various projects and sectors. Plans have been developed for the Han River Basin, Korea; Palawan, The Philippines; and Songkhla Lake Basin in Thailand, among others.

developmental project as compared to any natural changes which might occur.

The objective is to evaluate those changes in the environment induced by projects that affect human health and welfare either in the short or the long term. For example, industrial wastes may make water unsuitable for livestock, cutting mangroves for charcoal may ruin fish spawning grounds and thus reduce catches, or power plant emissions may cause an increased incidence of lung disease. Other effects have more indirect consequences on human welfare – conversion of forests to agricultural land may endanger wild species and reduce genetic diversity. The essence of environmental assessment is the prediction of alternative future states of resources and environment which will result from the choice of development path (including the option of no development at all).

Examples

A MULTIPURPOSE DAM PROJECT

Consider a plan to build a multipurpose dam. Conventional analysis would concentrate on the dam, the reservoir, the irrigated land and the production of electricity. The benefits of the dam would be thoroughly evaluated: power, water storage, flood control, fisheries, recreation and irrigation. The costs would be those of construction, operation and maintenance together with some attention to resettling those people to be moved from the area to be inundated (see Figure 2).

However, the natural boundary of the project is the entire river basin and this should, wherever appropriate, be reflected in the analysis. The displaced people may move in a number of directions: to the steeper lands, to the now protected flood plain, or to the new lake shore. If the uplands already support people engaged in activities like logging, tree-crop cultivation and shifting agriculture, the arrival of the displaced lowlanders may produce the sort of pressure on resources that will lead to shorter fallow periods, farming of marginal lands and the penetration, by means of logging roads, of steeper and yet more erodable areas.

An increase in soil erosion is thus virtually certain. Some of the resulting sediment will be carried downstream to the new reservoir where it can cause damage by abrasion to hydroelectric turbine blades, and turbidity which

FIGURE 2: *Multipurpose Dam Project: Loss of Economic Development Opportunities*

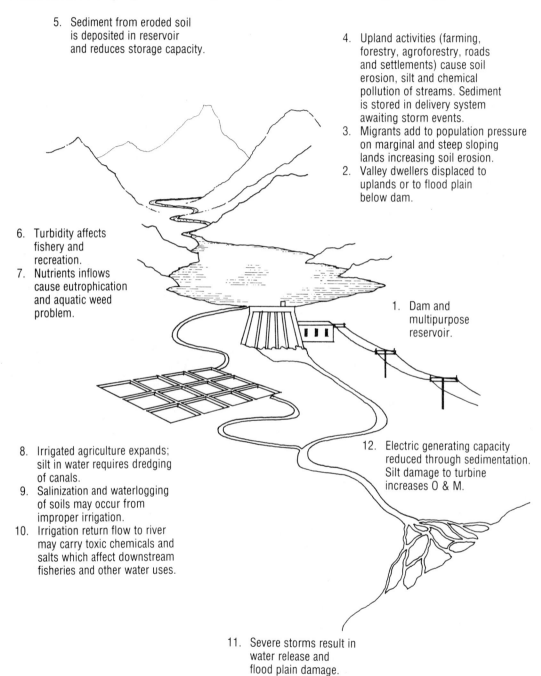

5. Sediment from eroded soil is deposited in reservoir and reduces storage capacity.

4. Upland activities (farming, forestry, agroforestry, roads and settlements) cause soil erosion, silt and chemical pollution of streams. Sediment is stored in delivery system awaiting storm events.

3. Migrants add to population pressure on marginal and steep sloping lands increasing soil erosion.

2. Valley dwellers displaced to uplands or to flood plain below dam.

6. Turbidity affects fishery and recreation.

7. Nutrients inflows cause eutrophication and aquatic weed problem.

1. Dam and multipurpose reservoir.

8. Irrigated agriculture expands; silt in water requires dredging of canals.

9. Salinization and waterlogging of soils may occur from improper irrigation.

10. Irrigation return flow to river may carry toxic chemicals and salts which affect downstream fisheries and other water uses.

12. Electric generating capacity reduced through sedimentation. Silt damage to turbine increases O & M.

11. Severe storms result in water release and flood plain damage.

may interfere with fish spawning. Nutrients washed out of the uplands may fertilize the growth of aquatic weeds which, as they die and decompose, reduce the dissolved oxygen in the water and thereby adversely affect fish production. Ultimately the sediment displaces the water in the reservoir, directly decreasing its storage capacity and reducing the useful life of the generating facility.

A reduction in the storage capacity of the reservoir due to sedimentation means that less storm water can be intercepted by the dam. In periods of heavy rain the spillways must be opened, thus negating the promise of flood protection which originally attracted residents and investment to the flood plain.

Irrigation water is delivered to fields under intensive agriculture, which includes the use of fertilizers and chemical pesticides. The runoff and irrigation return flow to the lower river basin may be substantially contaminated and thus affect fisheries and plant growth in the estuary and delta regions, with a consequent loss of income for the local communities.

The numbers of migratory fish may be reduced because the dam prevents them from moving upstream to spawn. Downstream fisheries may also be affected by changes in the water temperature from the impoundment of the river. In addition, the changes in nutrient and sediment delivery as a result of the alteration in the hydrologic regime may adversely affect coastal mangrove forests and marine fisheries.

In short, the entire watershed and its people will have become dependent on a system of water management which did not last long and which no longer brings the expected benefits.

Such effects have already occurred in numerous multipurpose dam projects. For example, in power projects in both Fiji and Western Samoa service roads built for transmission equipment opened up formerly inaccessible forest and hence made possible both poaching and deforestation. Changes have also been documented in hydrological patterns, soil erosion, siltation and flooding with consequent losses in forestry, agricultural land, and fisheries. A reduction in the useful life of downstream hydropower facilities, loss of property and increased incidences of disease have also been observed.

In a hydropower project in Papua New Guinea, the river-driven generator was built in a catchment area already under heavy pressure from other development projects which had changed the area's hydrological patterns and increased soil erosion rates. As a result there have been instances of extreme river flows which brought heavy loads of silt which, in turn, have affected the operation of the power station. In this case neither the project's design nor the estimates of its useful life took into account the surrounding environmental conditions which, although not a consequence of the project, considerably affected its operation.

Similar problems have been reported with major dam projects in Latin America (for example, loss of genetic diversity, upper watershed encroachment and increased soil erosion) and Africa (for example, health problems associated with the reservoir of the Aswan dam project in Egypt or involuntary resettlement issues in other countries).

In other projects considerable progress has been made in alleviating these types of adverse effect. The Kirindi Oya Irrigation and Settlement Project in Sri Lanka, for example, was located in a watershed that was in good condition. To ensure that the watershed would not deteriorate and adversely affect the project, a watershed management covenant was written into the loan agreement. In phase two of the project, land-use studies and the declaration of a protected area to be used for a reservoir will help to ensure that water continues to be available.

These projects illustrate the necessity of natural systems analysis. Without it the chances are that externalities will not be recognized in sufficient time to take the least costly countermeasures, nor to calculate the trade-offs between prevention and acceptance of damage.

IRRIGATED AGRICULTURE: SOIL SALINIZATION AND EFFECTS ON HUMAN HEALTH

Soil salinity, which is often caused by poorly designed or mismanaged irrigation schemes, has undermined, to varying degrees, the productivity of much irrigated land. Excessive irrigation, inadequate drainage or inadequate quantities of water for effective flushing are the principal causes of soil salinization.

A systematic analysis of the sources of salt within an area being developed and of ways of removing it will often permit the prevention of salinization and thus avoid the subsequent costly rehabilitation programs. The salt balance equation is illustrated in Figure 3. The information needed in order to calculate the net change in salt content is not difficult to obtain. Once the factors are known, salinization may usually be reduced or prevented

FIGURE 3: *The Salt Balance*

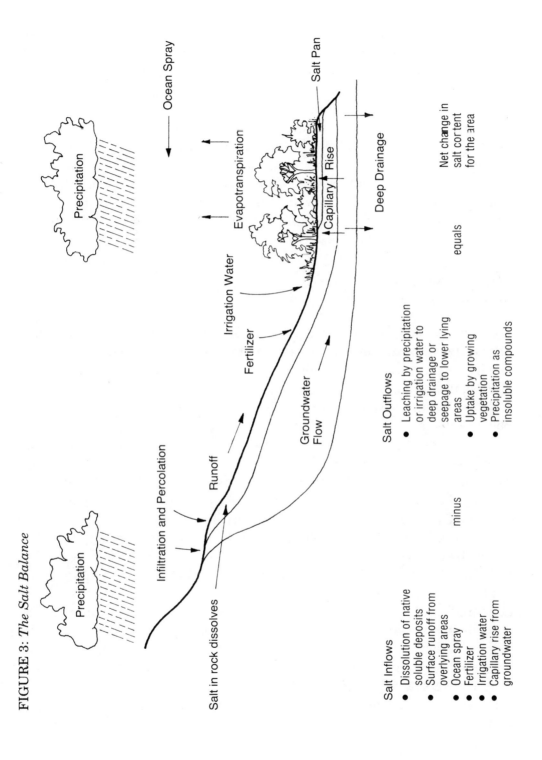

altogether by improving the design and management of irrigation systems to reduce salt inflows or increase salt outflows. The costs of such measures can then be compared to the benefits of greater agricultural production on salt-free soil and the avoided costs of rehabilitation at a later date.

Other unintentional and unforeseen consequences of irrigation projects include the effects on human health. The construction of water impoundments for irrigation and for other purposes in areas with endemic water-related diseases (for example malaria, schistosomiasis) has increased levels of infection and created new areas of transmission. Physical measures, such as drainage, flow modification, the lining of irrigation canals and the use of molluscicides and insecticides, can be taken to render the habitat less suitable for disease vectors.

URBAN AND INDUSTRIAL DEVELOPMENT PROJECTS IN COASTAL ZONES

Coastal zones support a number of land uses including agriculture, fisheries, and settlements, and provide a base for transport and trade. As both urban and industrial uses of coastal zones increase, it is becoming clear that many of these uses are incompatible.

Table 1 links developmental activities in a coastal zone to their biophysical and socioeconomic consequences. It is relatively easy to construct such a diagram for a specific development like a harbor improvement or an industrial site, and this provides a framework for data collection. For example, dredge and fill activities lead to sedimentation which directly reduces the productivity of sedentary species of shellfish and, by damaging coral reefs, indirectly affects other fisheries. The damage to fisheries is exacerbated by water pollution from agriculture and industry, and turbidity caused by construction.

Coastal waters are the most productive of all marine areas and provide the basis for most of the world's fisheries. Their role goes beyond merely providing a location for fishing. Many species of fish and crustaceans are dependent on near-shore waters during at least part of their life cycle. Mangrove swamps and inshore waters, for example, provide nursery areas and breeding grounds for many species which are commercially exploited in deeper waters later in their lives.

Fish, as well as being an important export product, are a vital source of

Table 1: Linkage between Development Activities and their Physical, Ecological and Socioeconomic Consequences

Matrix headings:

II. PHYSICAL CHANGE — *THAT RESULT IN*

Physical change columns: Temperature · Dissolved Oxygen · Nutrients · Salinity · Hydrology/Oceanography · Siltation/Sedimentation · Water Pollution/Toxic Subs · Pathologic Substances · Physical Disruption · Soil Erosion · Debris and Solid Wastes · Change in Cover · Overexploitation · Disruption of Migration · Disturbance of Behaviour · Overloading Encroachment

1. DEVELOPMENT ACTIVITY . . . CAUSES →

MANAGED ECOSYSTEM
- Agriculture and Farming
- Forestry
- Ranching and Feedlots
- Aquaculture and Mariculture
- Nearshore – Catch Fisheries

CONSTR. & TRANSPORT. FACILITIES
- Dredge-and-Fill Activities
- Airfields
- Causeways and Highways
- Harbours
- Shipping

INDUSTRIAL AND RELATED DEV.
- Military Facilities
- Electric Power Generation
- Heavy Industry
- Offshore Gas and Oil Development
- Coastal Mining
- Upland Mining

URBAN AND RESORT DEVELOPMENT
- Sanitary Sewage Discharges
- Solid Waste Disposal
- Water Development and Control
- Shoreline Management and Use
- Land Clearing and Site Preparation
- Coastal Resource Uses

III. ECOLOGICAL CONSEQUENCES · **IV. SOCIOECONOMIC CONSEQUENCES**

Socioeconomic consequence columns: Reduced Export Earnings Potential · Reduced Incomes for Commercial and Artisanal Fishermen · Reduced Availability of Protein Source · Increased Underemployment and Unemployment in Rural Areas · Increased Incidence of Human Disease

Ecological Consequence	Reduced Export Earnings Potential	Reduced Incomes for Commercial and Artisanal Fishermen	Reduced Availability of Protein Source	Increased Underemployment and Unemployment in Rural Areas	Increased Incidence of Human Disease
Biological Displacement/Change in Species Composition	•	•	•	•	
Lowered Species Diversity		•			
Reduction of Standing Stock	•	•	•		
Reproduction/Recruitment Failure	•	•			
Overutilization of Selected Species	•	•		•	
Smothering of Sedentary Species		•			
Mass Kills	•	•	•		
Respiratory Stress					
Inhibition of Photosynthesis		•			
Food Claim Concentration					•
Diseases of Stocks					•
Habitat Modification/Destruction	•	•	•	•	

Source: R.A. Carpenter (ed.), *Natural Systems for Development: What Planners Need to Know* (New York: Macmillan, 1983).

animal protein in most developing countries. The artisanal fisheries and the small-scale fish-processing factories are also important sources of income in many coastal areas. Any reduction in the productivity of fisheries therefore, has considerable socioeconomic consequences. Integrated analyses of coastal zones can reveal the impact of development projects upon the affected natural systems and allow the evaluation of the associated socioeconomic losses.

AIR POLLUTION FROM INDUSTRIAL FACILITIES

Air which is polluted by industry can seriously affect people as well as crops, livestock and materials. Pollution damage may occur at some distance from the source because its distribution depends on the vagaries of wind and terrain. Since emission controls are usually more costly to install after the initial design and construction of an industrial facility, it is important that they be included during the early stages of project planning and design.

One valuable tool for estimating the effects of emissions from plants such as coal-fired power stations or fertilizer manufacturing plants is the definition of an air quality control region (AQCR). Its boundaries are set either by measuring ambient conditions at a number of distances and directions from an existing source of pollution or by producing models which predict the dispersal of pollution from some future source, taking into account terrain, wind, temperature and plume characteristics. Population centers, transportation networks, topographical features and sensitive areas are all located. The patterns of pollution generation and their possible combinations are set out in the model for each major pollutant and atmospheric movement, and human activities are also included.

Although local governments are frequently responsible for setting the boundaries of the AQCRs and for determining emissions limits, similar assessments should be made for all project alternatives to assess the probable costs of pollution abatement.

Figure 4 shows how an AQCR is defined. The example is that of quarries near Kuala Lumpur, Malaysia, which produce a dust fall that adversely affects surrounding living quarters, farm animals, a temple and nature reserves.

FIGURE 4: *Dust Fall Concentration near Batu Caves, Kuala Lumpur, Malaysia, 1973–5 (in metric tons/km²/month)*

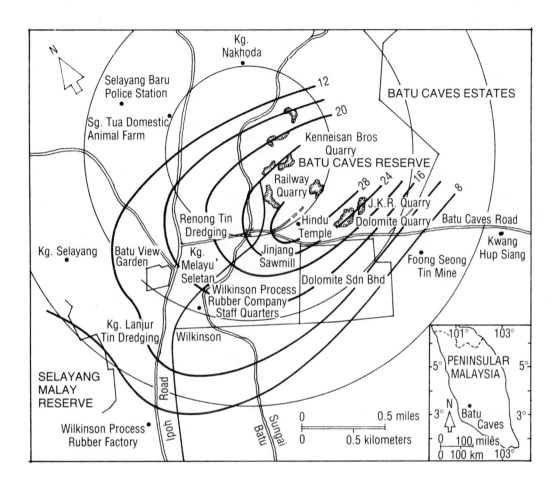

Source: R.A. Carpenter (ed.), *Natural Systems for Development: What Planners Need to Know* (New York: Macmillan, 1983).

Summary

A variety of approaches exist to identify and quantify the impacts of development projects on the environment and natural resources. These techniques, used together with an understanding of the geophysical setting of development projects, provide critical inputs into the economic analysis by focusing attention on other activities, both present and future, that may interact with the project at issue.

The essential point is that projects should not be considered in isolation from other human activities, nor from the dynamics of the neighboring environment. The biophysical description, together with the socioeconomic variables, form the basis of the economic evaluation of the costs and benefits of any given project.

3 *Economic measurement of impacts on the environment – theoretical basis and practical applications*

Both economic and financial analyses are commonly employed in project evaluation. Whereas financial analyses focus primarily on market prices and cash flows, economic analyses should include the benefits and costs of the effects that development projects have on the environment, whether or not they are reflected in the marketplace.[1]

Neoclassical Welfare Economics

It is useful to review the theoretical basis of economic, as opposed to financial, analysis. Neoclassical welfare economics, as developed by Pigou (1920) and Hicks (1939) among others, is concerned with the total welfare of society and evaluates alternative projects or actions on the basis of changes in social welfare. A number of important assumptions are implicit in this approach. These include:

(i) Societal welfare is the sum of individual welfare;

(ii) Individual welfare can be measured (measurement was originally conceived in terms of units of utility called "utiles" and, more conveniently, as reflected in the prices paid for goods and services); and

(iii) Individuals maximize their welfare by choosing that combination of goods, services and savings that yields the largest possible sum of total utility given their income constraints.

[1] For a full discussion of the roles of and the distinctions between economic and financial analysis, see Dixon and Hufschmidt (eds), *Economic Valuation Techniques for the Environment*, Chapter 2.

Of particular importance when valuing environmental effects subject to an income constraint are the following assumptions:

(i) Utility and welfare can be obtained from goods and services even if they are provided free or at minimum cost. The difference between the amount paid for a good or service, and the total utility enjoyed, is called "consumer's surplus" or CS.[1] Total utility for any good is the combination of the amount paid for the good plus any consumer's surplus. Graphically, this relationship can be derived from total utility and marginal utility curves and the related, easily observed, individual demand curve (graphs 1, 2, and 3, respectively, in Figure 5). As illustrated in the third graph in Figure 5, the area of consumer's surplus for good X is area PAB when the price is at P and the individual purchases quantity Y. If good X were free (price = 0), the entire area OAC would be consumer's surplus and would measure the benefit to the individual from consuming good X. Since many environmental goods and services have low or zero prices, the CS component in total utility of those goods and services may be very large. In turn, if these "free" environmental goods and services are lost, the loss of welfare (CS) is large.

(ii) Initially, we assume that the marginal utility of income is the same for all individuals. This means that all individuals get the same amount of increased utility from an additional dollar of income. This is obviously a very strong assumption and one that has to be relaxed in many situations. The discussion of the impact of development projects on income distribution mentioned in Chapter 1 is part of this issue. The assumption of a common marginal utility of income allows aggregation across individuals and the use of prices observed in one part of the economy to place values on unpriced goods and services that may occur elsewhere. To aggregate individual demand curves into market demand curves, we need either no change in income distribution or an income elasticity of demand which is the same for all individuals.

In reality, the marginal utility of income usually decreases as income increases. That is, the utility from an extra dollar's income

---

[1] CS can be measured in two ways: compensating variation (CV) and equivalent variation (EV). These measures are discussed in Chapter 6.

FIGURE 5: *Total and Marginal Utility Curves and Individual Demand Curve for Good X*

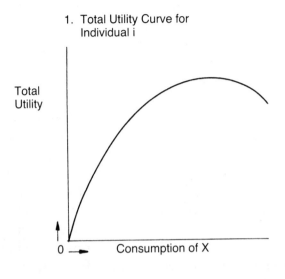

1. Total Utility Curve for Individual i

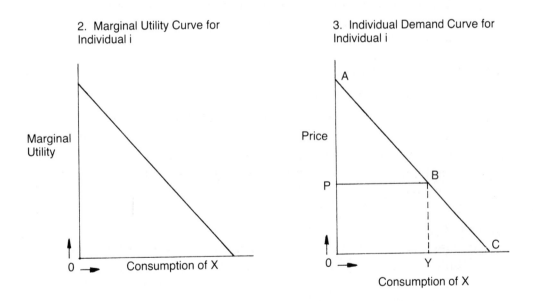

2. Marginal Utility Curve for Individual i

3. Individual Demand Curve for Individual i

for a rich person is less than that for a poorer individual. In practice we cannot compare utility across individuals, so for simplification we assume a constant marginal utility of income. One way to avoid the implications of this assumption is the use of "weights". This topic will be discussed further in Chapter 7.

(iii) Total individual welfare (and, in turn, societal welfare) is equal to the sum of expenditures and consumer's surplus. Both of these components are appropriate indicators of welfare and should be measured and included in the analysis.

(iv) Using "willingness to pay" measures in benefit-cost analysis implies two value judgements: individual preferences count; and individual preferences should be weighted by some factor correlated with income, either the status quo or by some other criterion.

The implications of the previous assumptions have frequently been overlooked. Project analyses have usually focused on the easily measured direct benefits and costs (also used in financial analyses) and often ignore the economic externalities – some of which may be measured directly by using market prices, but many of which consist of losses (or, more rarely, gains) of consumer's surplus.

This book focuses on techniques for measuring environmental externalities so that a comprehensive social welfare analysis may be undertaken.

Practical Applications

To conduct the expanded economic analysis advocated here, the analyst has to accept both the implications derived from welfare economics and the need for multidisciplinary work. It would be unusual for any one person to have the necessary breadth of knowledge to assess properly both the "economic" and "environmental" effects of any given project. The role of the environmental specialist in helping to identify these effects was discussed in Chapter 2. This book will not discuss this topic further, but the importance of multidisciplinary work cannot be overstated.

The hardest task for the economist or project analyst is to decide which of the environmental and resource impacts to include and then how to quantify and monetize them. There is no "cookbook" answer, yet the analysis should not be done *ad hoc*. Our approach is one which requires the analyst to think through each problem, identify important impacts, make decisions, and make all assumptions explicit. Some general guidelines that should be of help in setting up the analysis follow:

(i) *Start simply with the most obvious, most easily valued environmental impacts*. This may mean looking for impacts on the environment resulting in changes in productivity that can be valued using market prices. A mining operation, for example, may disrupt a traditional downstream fishery or some agricultural activity. The net change in fish or crop production can be identified and valued. The change in the quantity and quality of water flowing downstream and its effect on the coastal mangroves or on offshore coral reefs is a secondary effect. Secondary effects may be very important, both ecologically and economically, but the analyst would do best to start with the fishery or the agricultural activity. In short, start with the effects that have directly measurable productivity changes that can be valued by market prices.

(ii) There is a useful symmetry in benefits and costs: a benefit forgone is a cost, while a cost avoided is a benefit. The analyst should always look at both the benefit and cost sides of any action and approach valuation in the most feasible and cost-effective way. The value of improved industrial waste water treatment should be approached from both the direct cost side (largely capital and operation, maintenance and replacement costs) and the "costs avoided" side – the benefits of reduced downstream water purification costs or reduced morbidity. The distinction between benefits (costs avoided) and costs is the reference point from which changes are measured. If a decision is made to take some action (for example, pollution control) even though the benefits are not measured, the approach is a form of cost-effectiveness analysis which is discussed in Chapter 4.

(iii) Just as many impacts on environment and resources can be analyzed from either the benefit or the cost side, the economic analysis itself should be done in a *with-and-without-project framework*. It is important that only additional or incremental benefits and costs due to implementation of the project be considered. Sunk costs – costs already spent directly or indirectly on the project – should not be included. A series of alternative "with-project" options (for example, varying scale) may need to be considered.

(iv) *All assumptions should be stated explicitly*. This is particularly important in valuing effects on the environment because other analysts may wish to challenge the results and can do so only if the assumptions and the data are clearly presented.

(v) When market prices cannot be used directly, it may be possible to use them indirectly by means of *surrogate-market techniques*. In these approaches, the market prices of substitute or complementary goods are used to value an unpriced environmental good or service. For example, the value of an unpriced environmental amenity, such as clean air, may be a factor in the price of marketable assets, such as housing or land. Analysis of the price differentials of such assets in areas of varying air quality may give an indication of an implicit price for the unpriced environmental amenity.

Table 2 gives a matrix of typical development projects and the basic measurement and valuation approaches which are described in Chapters 4, 5 and 6. Each cell lists representative impacts on the environment that might be valued by means of various methods. Much can be done by using data on quantity and prices that are fairly easy to observe or to obtain. Frequently the hardest step is to ask the right questions. The projects listed are only a sample; many more types of project and their impacts could be added.

The choice of a particular method of measurement will obviously depend on what is being measured. None the less, in Table 2 there are some methods which are listed quite frequently: changes in productivity and cost-effectiveness, for example, are cited several times. Although a wide range of measurement/valuation techniques have been developed by economists, this book will concentrate on those which are more easily applied to the probable environmental effects of standard types of development projects.

Table 3 lists these techniques by chapter. The first set, those thought to be generally applicable, are presented in Chapter 4. These are fairly standard and straightforward approaches that rely largely on changes in physical production or on direct cash expenditures (for example, preventive expenditure, cost-effectiveness). Opportunity-cost and loss-of-earnings approaches look at economic costs associated with environmental impacts. These approaches provide powerful tools for measuring many of the effects that development projects have on the environment.

A second set of techniques, presented in Chapter 5, are "potentially" applicable because they can be used only in certain situations. These approaches are usually more indirect and rely either on surrogate markets (for example travel costs, property values, land values) or the costs involved in relocating and replacing facilities. The scope for using both sets of techniques is elaborated in the text.

Chapter 6 presents information on survey-based, contingent-valuation approaches and the use of macroeconomic models. Although these approaches have more limited immediate usefulness in many developing countries, there are cases when such approaches can be, and have been, used.

Besides the major task of identifying the impacts on the environment and determining their monetary values, three important conceptual problems remain: determining the *boundary* of the analysis; setting an appropriate *time horizon*, and choosing a *technique* for project evaluation.

The "boundary" of the economic analysis refers to the choice of what to include and what to exclude. The identification of externalities implies an expansion of the conceptual and physical boundaries of the analysis. How far to expand will depend on each individual project. An oil palm mill will generate waste water which will adversely affect downstream uses of water – including drinking, irrigation and fishing. We will argue that the economic analysis of the project should include these effects in a with-and-without-project framework.

Other impacts on the environment may be more distant or more difficult to identify. The effect of emissions from a power plant on creation of acid rain is one example. The interaction of upland agricultural development with its attendant soil and chemical runoff, and lowland and coastal ecosystems provide another example of a complicated, extended relationship. No single rule can be used to draw lines for the analysis. As with valuation, we believe that it is best to start with the directly observable and measurable effects. The project engineer, the economic analyst and the environmental specialist will collectively have to determine the boundaries. In time it may be possible to determine "protocols" for representative types of project; each protocol would outline the impacts on the environment likely to be produced by given projects which should be considered in the analysis. A significant contribution to the development of such protocols would be the results of *ex post facto* evaluations of similar projects as well as the checklists and guidelines developed by environmental specialists.

Setting an appropriate *time horizon* is the next major conceptual problem.

Table 2: Examples of Development Projects, Possible Environmental Impacts and Measurement and Valuation Techniques

Type of project	Environmental impacts	Measurement and valuation techniques/comments
Agriculture, Forestry, and Fisheries Development		
Fertilizer factory	Project designed for solid, liquid, and gaseous waste treatment.	*Cost-effectiveness* of alternative treatment designs.
Hill forest development	Project will increase fuelwood and fodder production, and protect critical watershed.	*Change in productivity* of forests and agricultural land. *Opportunity cost* of dung as fertilizer to value benefit of alternative fuel. *Opportunity cost* of preserving critical watershed.
Fisheries development	Project contributes to overexploitation of shrimp resources. Project vessels competing with artisanal fishermen – project catch not fully incremental. Evidence of overfishing inshore.	*Change in productivity* of fishery due to overfishing. *Loss of earnings* of artisanal fishermen must be subtracted from project catch projections.
Brackish-water shrimp culture	Removal of mangroves for construction of shrimp ponds.	*Change in productivity* of fishery due to mangrove removal.
Livestock development	Effects on forests and range land of overgrazing.	*Change in productivity* of forests and range land. *Opportunity cost* of dung as fertilizer.
Irrigation		
Low-lift pump maintenance	Shallow flooded areas overdrained resulting in lack of water for surface water irrigation in dry season.	*Change in productivity* due to moisture deficit in dry season.
Irrigation and settlement	Project located in watershed in good condition; there should therefore be low sedimentation rate.	Watershed management covenant in loan agreement to assure that increased development resulting in increased sedimentation would not affect project's future operation.
Outfall drain	Project should have positive environmental impacts by correcting waterlogging and soil salinization problems.	*Change in productivity* from better growing conditions. *Cost-effectiveness* of alternative rehabilitation designs.
Infrastructure		
Road development in hilly area	New cuts in embankments not stabilized with vegetation, causing potential for soil erosion and landslides.	*Change in productivity* due to soil erosion and sedimentation. *Loss of property* due to landslides.

Urban water supply	Project contributed to increased waste-water volume without providing adequate sewerage facilities.	*Loss of earnings* directly due to flooding or indirectly as a result of increased incidence of waterborne disease. *Loss of property* due to flooding.
Provincial cities water supply	Watershed denudation in the upper recharge area of the project affects project performance.	The broader issue of management of watershed on which the project depends should have been given consideration.
Water supply	Water diverted from downstream users by artificial well recharge in river bed.	*Change in productivity* of downstream water users.
Low-income urban housing	Increased air pollution due to use of underfloor heating systems burning soft-coal briquettes.	*Cost-effectiveness* of alternative heating designs. *Loss of earnings* from increased respiratory diseases.
Industry and power Gas turbine generation	Designed as peak-load facility to run on gas. No air quality control included in design. Was used as base-load facility run on oil. Air quality adversely affected by emissions.	*Cost-effectiveness* of alternative designs to decrease emissions.
Palm oil processing plant	Untreated effluent with BOD of 20 000 mg/l discharged into river.	*Change in productivity* of inland fishery due to water pollution. *Cost-effectiveness* of alternative water-treatment designs. *Loss of earnings* from increased health problems due to use of polluted water.
Tin mining	Environmental aspects given due consideration with respect to waste tailing disposal, water storage pond dike burst prevention, and prevention of malaria-mosquitoes breeding.	Project accounted for major potential environmental problems. Negative environmental impact should be minimal.
Hydropower development project	Service roads gave access which promoted deforestation resulting in changes in hydrological patterns, soil erosion, siltation and flooding.	*Change in productivity* of forests, agricultural land, and downstream fishery. Reduction in useful life of downstream hydropower facility. *Loss of earnings* as a direct result of flooding or indirectly as a result of increased incidence of disease.
Hydropower development project	Run-of-river power facility located in catchment with heavy development pressure resulting in increased extreme river flow rates and heavy siltation loads.	Project design and estimates of project's useful life should account for surrounding environmental conditions which will affect project operation even though not a direct consequence of project. *Preventive expenditures* made to reduce downstream consequences of deforestation.

Table 3: Measurement and Valuation Techniques

Generally Applicable (Chapter 4)

---

1. Those that use the market value of directly related goods and services:
    (i) Changes-in-productivity approaches
    (ii) Loss-of-earnings approaches
    (iii) Opportunity-cost approach

2. Those that use the value of direct expenditures:
    (i) Cost-effectiveness analysis
    (ii) Preventive expenditures

Potentially Applicable (Chapter 5)

---

1. Those that use surrogate-market values:
    (i) Property-value approach
    (ii) Other land-value approaches
    (iii) Wage-differential approach
    (iv) Travel-cost approach
    (v) Marketed goods as environmental surrogates

2. Those that use the magnitude of potential expenditures:
    (i) Replacement costs
    (ii) Relocation costs
    (iii) Shadow-project approach

Survey-Based Methods and Macroeconomic Models (Chapter 6)

---

1. Contingent valuation methods:
    (i) Bidding games
    (ii) Take-it-or-leave-it experiments
    (iii) Trade-off games
    (iv) Costless choice
    (v) Delphi technique

2. Macroeconomic models:
    (i) Input–output models
    (ii) Linear programming models

Usually the time chosen should be long enough to encompass the useful life of the proposed investment – thus a factory will have a defined "life of project". In other kinds of project in which benefits are expected to accrue over very long periods (for example, a dam or reservoir with a life expectancy of some three hundred years) a time horizon is chosen which will capture most of the benefits and costs – say some thirty to fifty years. At any positive discount rate the present-day magnitudes of benefits and costs will, after fifty years, be very small in the calculations of net present value. A discount rate of ten percent, for instance, would mean that most benefits and costs would become inconsequential after only twenty years. (Discounting and discount rates will be discussed later in this chapter.)

The environmental impacts of development pose a special challenge. If the duration of the impact is less than the expected economic life of the project, then there is no problem – the effects on the environment can be included in the standard economic analysis. For example, an oil palm plantation with a project life expectancy of twenty-five years may involve road construction during its initial phase. The construction of the roads causes an increase in soil erosion, with consequent sedimentation downstream in an irrigation canal. After five years the road cuts have been stabilized, erosion has stopped and extra costs for dredging the canal have come to an end. In such a case the project's impacts on the environment can be included in the standard analysis.

If, on the other hand, the effects on the environment are expected to last beyond the lifetime of the funded project, the time horizon over which the project must be considered must be extended. For example, consider a new port to be developed by means of dredging. The process is expected to destroy an established fish breeding ground and its associated fishery. The port project is expected to last for twenty-five years and is evaluated over that period. However, as the fishery will never be re-established, its loss of fish production beyond the twenty-five years should also be included in the analysis.

There are two ways in which the extended time horizon to be considered can be accommodated within an analysis. One is to *extend the cash-flow analysis* beyond the normal end-of-project period for an additional number of years. This course is feasible if what is being considered has a clearly defined expected life (a teak forest, once cut, may need sixty years to regenerate, for example). The second way is to add a *capitalized value* of net benefits (or costs) at the normal end of the project period. This approach implicitly assumes that the impact on the environment (either a benefit or a cost) extends to infinity. In essence the second method is the establishment of a kind of "environmental salvage value" for the project and is likely to be a negative – although it can be a positive – number. As with the determination of the analytical boundary, the setting of the appropriate period is a multidisciplinary task which will require the cooperation of various specialists.

Beyond all this there are some impacts on the environment which are almost impossible to quantify and sometimes even difficult to identify. Aesthetic, sociocultural and historical factors are all examples of intractable types of impacts. Effects on genetic diversity and gene pools present similar problems. Such factors may be important, but they are not easily handled by economic analysis. They are discussed in Chapter 7.

Once the appropriate conceptual and temporal analytical boundaries have been set for a project, the next step is the choice of technique for evaluation. Three methods are commonly used for comparing costs and benefits: the internal rate of return (IRR) or economic internal rate of return (EIRR), the benefit/cost ratio (BCR), and net present value (NPV).

All three evaluation criteria depend on the same information – the yearly generation of benefits and costs associated with the project over the appropriate time horizon. Box 1 presents some basic information on the three criteria; they are also covered in detail in any standard project evaluation text (for example Gittinger, 1982; Mishan, 1982).

BOX 1: CRITERIA FOR PROJECT EVALUATION

Perhaps the single most widely used formula in project analysis is that which calculates the *net present value* (NPV) of a project. Also known as net present worth, the NPV determines the present value of net benefits by discounting the streams of benefits (B) and costs (C) back to the beginning of the base year (t = 1). Two formulas can be used; both yield identical results:

$$NPV = \sum_{t=1}^{n} \frac{B_t - C_t}{(1 + r)^t}$$

or

$$NPV = \sum_{t=1}^{n} \frac{B_t}{(1 + r)^t} - \sum \frac{C_t}{(1 + r)^t}$$

The *internal rate of return* (IRR) is defined as the rate of return on an investment which will equate the present value of benefits and costs. It is found by an iterative process and is equivalent to the discount rate (r) that satisfies the following relationship:

$$\sum_{t=1}^{n} \frac{B_t - C_t}{(1 + r)^t} = 0$$

or

$$\sum_{t=1}^{n} \frac{B_t}{(1 + r)^t} = \sum_{t=1}^{n} \frac{C_t}{(1 + r)^t}$$

The IRR is widely used by financial institutions, but there are some theoretical and practical problems associated with its usage. These are discussed in Hufschmidt *et al.* (1983), pp. 41–3.

The IRR is the discount rate that would result in a zero net present value for a project. If the IRR calculated is 15 percent and the cost of project funds is 10 percent, the project would be financially attractive. If project funds "cost" 18 percent, however, the project would be financially unattractive. The IRR does not give one the discount rate; it merely finds the value of r that meets the set condition of a zero net present value. The calculated IRR must then be compared to some other financial interest rate or discount rate to determine whether the project is financially or economically attractive.

The *benefit-cost ratio* (B/C ratio) is a simple derivative of the net present value criterion:

$$\text{B/C ratio} = \frac{\displaystyle\sum_{t=1}^{n} \frac{B_t}{(1 + r)^t}}{\displaystyle\sum_{t=1}^{n} \frac{C_t}{(1 + r)^t}}$$

This ratio compares the discounted benefits to discounted costs. If the B/C ratio is exactly equal to 1, the project will produce zero net benefits over its lifetime – the discounted benefits just equal discounted costs. A B/C ratio of less than 1 means that the project generates losses from an economic perspective.

Adapted from Dixon and Hufschmidt (eds) (1986), pp. 46–7.

Both NPV and B/CR require that a discount rate be chosen. The determination of this rate for development projects is a policy decision and detailed discussion of it is therefore beyond the scope of this book. However, important factors governing the choice of a discount rate include the opportunity cost of capital, the social rate of time preference, the requirements of the donor or lending agency, and the developing country's view of the consumption-investment mix of the private and public sectors. Box 2 presents additional information on discount rates.

BOX 2: DISCOUNT RATES

Whereas in financial analysis the interest rate used normally reflects market rates for investment and working capital and is therefore sensitive to current or expected inflation rates, the discount rate used in economic analysis is usually not readily observable in the economy. Economists have developed a number of approaches for determining and justifying a discount rate.

In the *Guide* and other references (Gittinger, 1982; Baumol, 1968) several explanations are given of possible choices of a discount rate for use in economic analysis. They are all based on economic or social phenomena:

OPPORTUNITY COST OF CAPITAL

This approach is based on the forgone production that results when capital is invested in one project rather than another, or invested in a particular project by government rather than by the private sector. In this sense the opportunity cost of capital is directly related to the theory of capital productivity. Invested in plant or equipment, a dollar's worth of investment should yield net benefits over time. The discount rate reflects this rate of return.

This approach is also closely related to the financial (or nominal) interest rate, although the latter may include an upward adjustment for inflation. The real (inflation-adjusted) opportunity-cost rate is affected by changes in real income, the distribution of wealth, taste, and technology (Hyman and Hufschmidt, 1983).

The opportunity-cost approach appears to be used (implicitly) by many international development banks in requiring that, to be eligible for loans, proposed projects promise an annual rate of return at least equal to a specified rate – which appears to be based on the opportunity cost of capital.

THE COST OF BORROWING MONEY

Governments frequently have to borrow money, either domestically or internationally, to finance development projects. The financing mechanisms used include government debt from borrowing, inflation, or taxation on private consumption (Haveman, 1969). Especially when a country expects to borrow abroad, this approach may be used to set the discount rate.

A danger in this cost-of-borrowing-money criterion is that extremely favorable loans (at very low, subsidized interest rates) will favor projects with long-term net benefits and conversely, a high discount rate will favor short-term-pay-off projects. To the extent that these extremes represent distortions of true scarcity in the economy, they will lead to misallocation of scarce resources.

THE SOCIAL RATE OF TIME PREFERENCE

A third school of thought relies on the ability of society to reflect more accurately than the private market the trade-offs between present and future consumption. If, from society's viewpoint, individuals overconsume in the present rather than save for investment and increased future production, the social rate of time preference will lead to a lower discount rate than that exhibited by individuals in private markets (the lifetime of an individual is much shorter than the relevant time horizon of society). How this rate is actually set depends upon the circumstances in the particular country involved. If the social rate is determined by the political process, this in turn is influenced by elected officials who may have a very short time horizon – namely, until the next election.

In summary, the actual rate to be used in economic analysis will be country-specific and will probably be established as a matter of government policy. Important factors governing the choice of rate will be the opportunity cost of capital, donor or lending agency requirements, cost of money to the government, and government's current views of the private-sector consumption-investment mix in relation to its concerns for future generations. The following points are important:

- Only one discount rate will be used in any single economic analysis, although the analysis may be repeated several times using different discount rates (sensitivity analysis).
- The discount rate used does not reflect inflation; all prices used in the analysis are real or constant dollar prices.
- In theory, the discount rate can be positive, zero, or negative; ignoring the concept of discounting (in effect, adapting a zero discount rate) does not do away with the problem of trade-offs between present and future consumption (time preference).

When in doubt, project analysts should seek guidance from responsible government policy-making agencies on the discount rate to be used. In the absence of such guidance, analysts should undertake project economic analyses using a range of rates reflecting those recently or currently in use in the country for public and private investment projects. It is important to re-emphasize that these rates should be on a real-cost, inflation-adjusted basis.

Adapted from Dixon and Hufschmidt (eds) (1986), pp. 43–5.

The EIRR technique does not require the pre-selection of a discount rate, but in effect it calls for a very similar sort of judgement, since a particular interest rate or discount rate is used as a cut-off point for determining the economic attractiveness of the project at issue.

In the case of many development banks (including the ADB and the World Bank), it is standard to use EIRR with a cut-off rate of 10 percent to 12 percent to determine the economic attractiveness of a project. In other funding agencies, the NPV or B/C ratio criterion is commonly used. Although all three criteria are based on the same data, if multiple projects are being considered the different criteria may yield different rankings. The B/C ratio, for example, focuses on the generation of benefits per unit of costs, not on the absolute magnitude of net benefits generated. The NPV criterion, on the other hand, measures the overall size of net benefits (contributions to social welfare) generated by a project. A fuller discussion of this topic is presented in Gittinger (1982) and Dixon and Hufschmidt (1986).

4 *Generally applicable techniques*

This chapter presents five generally applicable valuation techniques. Each of these techniques is in common use. The selection of the appropriate technique will be influenced by many factors including the effect to be valued and the availability of data, time and financial resources. The challenge, as outlined in Chapters 2 and 3, is to identify the environmental effects of the projects concerned and to incorporate correctly the valuation of their benefits and costs within the project analysis.

All the techniques presented in this chapter use market prices to determine values. The implicit assumption, therefore, is that these prices reflect economic scarcity and hence are economic efficiency prices. If there are distortions in the market prices, then appropriate adjustments will be required. Distortions often arise as a result of taxes, subsidies, exchange rates, or mandated wage or interest rates. The derivation of adjusted prices (commonly called shadow prices) is discussed in detail in standard project analysis handbooks (for example, Squire and Van der Tak, 1975; Gittinger, 1982; Little and Mirrlees, 1974).

In this and the following chapters, each technique is described briefly and examples are provided. References to standard works which present fuller explanations of the approach are also included. The focus is on fairly simple techniques that are most easily applied given the data and time limitations common to project analysis.

Techniques in which Market Prices are Used to Value a Change in Production

The techniques discussed here are those of straightforward benefit-cost analysis. The emphasis, however, is on the economic valuation of the environmental impacts of development projects. Impacts on environmental quality or on the sustainability of renewable resources are frequently reflected in changes in productivity of the systems involved and these, in turn, are used to assign values. Many of the valuation techniques listed in Table 2 rely on market prices to determine values.

Both natural and human systems may be affected. Natural systems include fisheries, agriculture and forests; human systems would include buildings, materials and products both in the producer and household sectors, as well as health and productivity.

The sustainability of resource use and the quality of the environment are treated as factors of production. Changes in these factors often lead to changes in productivity and/or production costs which may, in turn, lead to changes in prices and levels of output which can be observed and measured. It is their dual nature that makes the techniques so attractive – physical changes in production are easily observed and measured, and the use of market prices avoids some of the difficult questions of valuation arising from environmental effects which are not marketed. Before market prices can be used to value changes in productivity, assumptions must be made about the relevant supply and demand curves. Two situations may be distinguished:

(i) If the increase (or decrease) in the output of a commodity is small relative to the total market for it, and the change of inputs is small relative to the market for variable factors, then it can be assumed that product and variable factor prices will remain constant after the change in production. This assumption is the simplest one since it does not need further assumptions about the direction and magnitude of price changes – this is the basic "small project" assumption. For most projects this partial equilibrium view is a realistic assumption and is used implicitly in most of the techniques presented here.

(ii) Sometimes, however, the change in output of a commodity will be large enough to affect either the output prices, factor prices, or both. In such cases, information is needed about the shape of both demand and supply curves and then appropriate adjustments need to be made (see the *Guide*, pp. 173–5).

Three sets of techniques are considered. Each set uses market prices to value a change in the production of some good or service. The first deals with *changes in productivity and the value of output*; the second with *loss of earnings*; the third with the *opportunity costs* of different actions.

CHANGES IN PRODUCTIVITY

Techniques using changes in productivity as the basis for measurement are direct extensions of traditional benefit-cost analyses. Physical changes in production are valued using market prices for inputs and outputs or, when distortions exist, appropriately modified market prices. The monetary values thus derived are then incorporated into the economic analysis of the project. This approach is based directly on neoclassical welfare economics and the determination of social welfare. The benefits and cost of an action are counted regardless of whether they occur within the project boundaries or beyond them.

Several steps must be taken in order to use this technique:

(i) Changes in productivity caused by the project have to be identified both on site and off site. Changes on site are typically the outputs for which the project was designed and are included in any project analysis. Changes off site (both positive and negative) include all the environmental or economic externalities which were frequently ignored in the past. These off-site effects must be included to give a true picture of project impacts.

(ii) The effects on productivity both of proceeding with the project and of not going ahead should be assessed. Even if alternative projects are being considered, the "without-project" option should be retained. The reason for this is simple: we have to be able to specify the changes which will be brought about by the project as compared to what would happen if no project were undertaken. For example, a proposed agricultural development project in an upland area may cause soil erosion and increase damages to irrigated rice fields downstream. The environmental "cost" of the project is not the total damage to the rice fields, but only that caused by the additional load of sediment produced by the project. An analysis which postulates both "with" and "without" scenarios will help to clarify the degree of damage or the damage avoided as a result of the project.

In the evaluation of the without-project alternative, care must be taken to account for what might be expected to occur without the project. In many cases, this will not be a simple continuation of current levels of output. If the resource would be expected to degrade over time if no action were taken, this decline over time must be taken into account. We want to compare the actual differences of the with-project and without-project alternatives over time, not just a comparison to the current situation.

(iii) Assumptions have to be made about the time over which the changes in productivity must be measured, the "correct" prices to use, and any future changes expected in relative prices.

An example of this approach, taken from a soil-conservation project in Nepal, is presented in the Appendix. In it, changes in the production of grass and fodder are valued in terms of the value of milk and dung produced by livestock. Other projects with adverse environmental impacts which can be valued using this method were listed in Table 2 and include projects in forestry, fisheries and agriculture as well as other sectors. Other examples include:

(i) In the construction of the Hetauda–Narayangard Road in Nepal the new road cuts were not stabilized with vegetation and were thus potential causes of soil erosion and landslides, thereby affecting agricultural productivity.

(ii) In a project for brackish-water fish culture in Thailand, the removal of mangroves for fish-pond construction could result both in decreased availability of mangrove products and of reduced inshore fish catches.

(iii) A palm oil processing plant in Indonesia releases its untreated effluent, with a high BOD content, into a river whose polluted waters then affect the productivity of a downstream fishery.

Many other examples exist, but they all have one common characteristic: designed for one particular purpose, each project causes unintentional damage to another productive system. The value of this unintended "cost" can be estimated by using the simple technique of valuing the change in productivity.

LOSS OF EARNINGS

This technique is similar to that for changes in productivity, except in this case changes in human productivity are measured. The lost earnings and medical costs that result from the environmental damage caused by a project, or the comparable savings which would accrue from preventing that damage, become the standard of valuation. Known also as the *human capital* or *forgone earnings* approach, these techniques pose some major ethical problems when applied to human life itself. We will avoid placing any monetary value either on life *per se* or on the psychological costs of illness and death.[1]

It is possible, however, to estimate the value of lost earnings and medical costs caused by changes in the quality of the environment (Freeman, 1979; Lave and Seskin, 1977).

Mishan (1982), Ridker (1967) and Kneese (1966) have all discussed aspects of the human capital approach. In its simplest form the stream of lost earnings and costs of health care due to environmental damage (for example, noise pollution, polluted air or water) are examined. Thorny moral and theoretical difficulties arise when periods of illness lengthen. Most people would agree that the main "costs" of a three-day influenza are fairly easy to determine (lost wages and medical costs) but when an illness stretches on for weeks, months or years or ends in death, then the summing up is more difficult.

We cannot say exactly where the cut-off point should be. In general it is easier to value environmental effects using the loss-of-earnings approach when the illness is relatively short, discrete and does not have negative long-term effects. Chronic illness is harder to handle.

An example where the loss-of-earnings approach might be useful is an urban water supply project which reduces the incidence of diarrhea. It is easy to establish the direct connection between polluted water and diarrhea and the disease is not, in general, life-threatening.

Some general guidelines for choosing projects for which the loss-of-earnings approach may be used include the following:

(i) A direct cause-and-effect relationship can be established and the etiology of the disease is clearly identifiable.

(ii) The illness is of short duration, not life-threatening and has no major long-term effects.

(iii) The precise economic value of earnings and medical care is known. Unemployed laborers or subsistence farmers, for example, present problems in this context since a "shadow price" for their earnings must be developed.

---

[1] For further discussion of this issue, see M.W. Jones-Lee, *The Value of Life: an Economic Analysis* (Chicago: University of Chicago Press, 1976).

Certain types of environmentally related disease are very difficult to value, so greater caution in using the loss-of-earnings approach is called for when the following conditions pertain:

(i) The etiology is not well established. For example, though we know that the level of SO_x emissions affects human health, we may not be able accurately to translate emissions into health consequences.

(ii) A large number of pollution sources make the relationship between cause and effect difficult to establish. The quality of air and of water are frequently cited examples of this difficulty. For example, emissions of particulate matter are a major environmental problem, but it is extremely difficult to assign a change in the levels of particulates to controls placed on a single, large, coal-fired power plant. There may be too many unknown factors, too much "noise" in the system, to establish the necessary link. In such cases it may be better to use the technique of cost-effectiveness discussed below.

(iii) If the disease is chronic or its effects are debilitating but not completely disabling, the valuation problem becomes complicated by issues of measurement. This is the case when the victim functions at less than full potential although seeming to be "healthy". Mal-nourishment and chronic parasitic infections commonly produce such effects.

In applying the loss-of-earnings approach the analyst needs to identify clearly the cause-and-effect relationship and its implications on net social welfare. Candidates for the use of this technique would include projects designed to improve public water supplies or waste disposal systems which will ultimately improve human health and productivity. The analyst must be careful in determining the net improvement in worker production or earnings (or the reduction in illness) and the net social costs of savings in medical care. For example, where the demand for medical services is less than or equal to the supply, the savings in medical care are less than the actual medical costs which have been avoided, since some facilities or services may go unused as a result even though there is a cost to supplying them. This is a short-run effect. If, on the other hand, the demand for medical services exceeds the supply, as it does in many developing countries, then the full value of the savings in medical services can be counted as a benefit.

It should be noted that the term "loss of earnings" used here refers to health-related morbidity or mortality. In Table 2 the same term is used in another sense: a loss of (income) earnings can also be caused by exogenous reductions in productivity in, say, a farmer's fields or in a fishery operation. This also represents a loss of welfare but a loss caused by external factors, not by a failure of physical well-being.

OPPORTUNITY COST

This approach is based on the concept that the cost of using resources for unpriced or unmarketed purposes (for example, preserving land for a national park rather than harvesting its trees for timber) can be estimated by using the forgone income from other uses of the resource as a proxy. Rather than attempting to measure directly the benefits gained from preserving a resource for these unpriced or unmarketed purposes, we measure what has to be given up for the sake of preservation. The opportunity-cost approach is, therefore, a way of measuring the "cost of preservation". This information, in turn, is used to evaluate the options open to a decision-maker. There are many instances where the opportunity cost of preservation is found to be low, resulting in a decision to preserve or to conserve the resource in its natural state.

The first step of the analysis is a conventional benefit-cost analysis of the proposed project. If the traditional project analysis shows the project to be uneconomic, the analysis need go no further. If, however, the proposed project does have positive net benefits, these must be weighed against the benefits of the preservation alternative which can be measured easily. If these measurable benefits of the preservation alternative outweigh the project benefits, the project should not be undertaken.

Where the benefits of the proposed project are slightly greater than the preservation alternative, we are left with a difficult choice. The preservation alternative will also have some less tangible benefits such as option value, quasi-option value and existence value (these are discussed in Chapter 7) which are not easily measured. These unquantified benefits must then be weighed qualitatively against the amount of benefits by which the proposed project exceeds the preservation alternative. When the difference in benefits between the two alternatives is low, prudence is advised since development projects usually have irreversible effects. However, such subjective decisions must be left to policy-makers; the economist can only lay out the relevant information.

One well-known example of the use of this technique is the Hell's Canyon Study in the United States of America (Krutilla, 1969; Krutilla and Fisher, 1985). It had been proposed to dam the canyon for the generation of hydroelectric power which would have altered, irrevocably, a unique area of wilderness. Rather than trying to value all the benefits of the canyon in its natural state, the analysts produced conventional benefit-cost analyses both of the proposed project and of its next cheapest alternative. The analysis showed that even under a variety of assumptions, the benefits of the project were not large enough to justify the irreversible loss of a unique natural area. The decision-makers chose not to build the dam since the opportunity cost of preservation – the additional expense of generating power from another source – was thought to be worth paying for the sake of preserving Hell's Canyon in its natural state.

Nominally, this technique is a cost-side approach, but it is actually used to evaluate the benefits of preservation, which are not themselves valued, by means of estimating the extra costs entailed in using an alternative. In this way it may be very useful in valuing unique natural resources whose benefits are difficult to identify, monetize, or both. Possible situations where this approach may be valuable include alteration of tropical rainforests, establishment and protection of wildlife sanctuaries, cultural or historical sites and natural vistas. The technique is relatively quick and straight-forward and provides information valuable to decision-makers and to the public.

In terms of development projects it can also be used when deciding where major infrastructure projects or industrial facilities are to be sited. New ports, airports and highways all frequently require the use of open, un-developed or sparsely developed areas. Where alternative locations exist, the opportunity-cost technique helps to clarify the additional costs of preserving one area over another.

Similarly, the effect on the environment of different technological options can be valued with this technique. For example, it is possible to choose between alternative ways of meeting the same need, such as cooling ponds or cooling towers for heated water, between overhead or underground facilities, between parking lots or parking structures, and so on. With this technique it is possible to quantify the extra costs involved in choosing an environmentally better, but more expensive, solution. Of course the final decision will always lie in the hands of the policy-maker, but the opportunity-cost approach is a powerful tool with which to illustrate the real cost differences between alternatives which may have very different impacts on the environment.

Techniques in which Market Prices are Used to Value Costs

The final two techniques in this chapter rely on the use of market prices to evaluate costs that are actually incurred. The first, cost-effectiveness analysis, is a widely used economic and engineering technique. The second is the technique of preventive expenditures which examines direct costs involved with certain actions. Note that neither approach attempts to estimate a monetary value for the benefits produced by the project. The project output or product is described in qualitative or physical terms. For both sets of cost-side approaches, therefore, the analyst must determine that the potential benefits justify the costs involved.

COST-EFFECTIVENESS ANALYSIS

When funds are limited, data inadequate, or the level of knowledge insufficient to establish the link between environmental damage and human health and welfare, it may sometimes be more useful first to set a goal and then analyze different means of achieving it. Conversely, if there is a certain level of funding available for a given project, then the policy-maker must decide which method of using those funds will be the most effective. Alternatively, it might be necessary to consider a number of goals and to decide which of them seems best after considering the cost of each. In all of these situations, cost-effectiveness analysis is involved. The major difference between it and other approaches is that no attempt is made to monetize benefits. Rather, the focus is entirely on meeting a predetermined standard or goal. A number of the projects listed in Table 2 could use this approach to evaluate alternative ways of meeting project goals.

Cost-effectiveness analysis is also appropriate for social programs dealing with health and population as well as for the analysis of environmental effects. In general, it is useful for all projects whose benefits are difficult to measure in monetary terms.

The first step in cost-effectiveness analysis is to fix a target. In the environmental field this may, for example, be a certain ambient quality, a maximum level of exposure to a waterborne disease agent or an emission standard for industrial facilities. The policy-maker must consider the possible trade-offs between different standards and the costs associated with achieving them. The standard economic principle normally applied to this kind of decision is the equation of marginal costs with marginal benefits, where standards are increased to the point at which the additional costs of raising the standard further are just equal to the additional benefits from raising the standard. However, when benefits are difficult or impossible to measure or monetize, this approach becomes primarily conceptual.

In many cases technology may dictate the options available for achieving a target: as standards for air quality become more stringent, the possible strategies for control become fewer. In cases where there are only a few alternatives with very different outcomes, analyzing the incremental cost of adopting one rather than another may provide a clear indication of which strategy it is sensible to adopt. Where there are many possibilities it may be more difficult to choose the sensible standard and the corresponding strategy for achieving it.

Sometimes optimization techniques that can handle multiple objectives, such as linear programming, may be used to help to set standards (Russell, 1973; Russell and Vaughan, 1976). These can simultaneously take into account the level of the primary output, the environmental considerations and the costs associated with alternative strategies.

Once a target or standard is chosen, cost-effectiveness analysis is carried out by examining the various means by which that target can be achieved. This may involve analyzing the capital and operating costs of different pollution-control technologies. In other projects it may be management practices which are the variables subject to change. Each project will involve different alternatives and must be dealt with differently. Analysts must ensure that a wide range of options is considered, but the basic goal is the same – identifying the least-cost alternative which will achieve the goal selected.

The *Guide* provides many examples of cost-effectiveness analyses (pp. 272–85). These include case studies of electric power plants, petroleum refineries, regional air quality and waterborne diseases.

Although cost-effectiveness analysis seems to be a straightforward economic (and engineering) approach, in practice there is wide scope for further analysis. One of the main reasons for this can be seen in the example considered below. Frequently, alternative strategies may achieve different levels of control. For instance, if the "target" level is an emission standard of no more than 100ppm and there are three technologies from which to choose, A, B and C, the cost-effectiveness analysis may yield the following information:

Technology	Installation Cost (million $)	Emission Level (PPM)
A	50	98
B	15	135
C	25	105

Technology A is the only one which meets the set standard; technology B is much cheaper to install, but is clearly inadequate. Technology C is the problem. It costs only half as much as A and falls short of the target by only a small amount. Which technology should be recommended? A strict regulatory approach might demand that A be adopted, even though C would save $25 million. Is the slight increase in emissions justified by the savings? The cost-effectiveness analysis should present these choices to the decision-maker and, as mentioned in Chapter 2, input from both economic and environmental analysts should be considered in reaching a decision. The choice will depend on the potential dangers of the higher rates of emission and on how much society can afford and is willing to pay to reach certain standards.

This last point, how much a society is able or willing to pay, has not previously been discussed, but is of considerable importance. Since cost-effectiveness analysis often does not even attempt to estimate the benefits derived from meeting a given standard or goal, it is possible that even the most cost-effective (or least-cost) option of meeting a strict standard is still too expensive. This is not an excuse for doing nothing, but suggests rather that the standard should be relaxed. Cost-effectiveness analysis can help in pointing this out too. The experience of other countries can be used as a guide to both the target level or standards for emissions, and for their expected costs.

Some general guidelines follow:

(i) Examine targets in a mix of countries, both developed and developing. Find out what levels the World Health Organization (WHO) recommends and how they are determined.

(ii) Evaluate the seriousness of the environmental impact which is to be controlled. Discover if it is life-threatening (for example mercury poisoning), a health hazard (for example dust and particulates) or merely a nuisance (for example certain noise levels).

(iii) Evaluate the effect of the most cost-effective method of control on the financial and economic return from the project. If the cost of the preferred choice is so great that the project will not be profitable, then the decision must be either not to go ahead or to reconsider the issue of pollution control. Determine the implications of canceling the project. Consider the probable effects of reducing the levels of pollution control. Establish what lessons can be learned from other countries which have faced the same problems.

(iv) Discover whether there is some compromise which will minimize environmental damage while still allowing the project at issue, or another project, to be built.

In sum, cost-effectiveness is a powerful tool but one which has to be applied carefully. Rigid adherence to a standard which is too strict or inappropriate can result in excessive control costs or even the cancellation of a project. Although such drastic measures may be necessary in some instances, in many cases some compromise can be developed to allow the project to go forward while still protecting the environment. Sensibly applied, cost-effectiveness analysis can be very helpful in providing environmental protection at a moderate cost while allowing development activities to continue.

PREVENTIVE EXPENDITURES

It is sometimes possible to establish the minimum value that an individual will put on the quality of his or her environment by determining just how much people are prepared to spend in preventing damage either to it or to themselves. This is also true of communities or nations. Valuation performed in this manner is known as the "preventive-expenditure" or "mitigative-expenditure" approach. It gives a minimum estimate for two reasons: actual expenditures may be constrained by income, or there may be an additional amount of consumer's surplus even after the preventive expenditure has been made. Whereas the cost-effectiveness approach examines the direct cost of meeting some predetermined target or standard, this technique examines actual expenditures in order to determine the importance individuals attach to impacts on the environment.

Theoretically, a rational individual would incur mitigating costs if:

$$N' + E < N$$

where N = original level of perceived damage

N′ = mitigated level of perceived damage

E = mitigation expenditure

It is also thought that a rational individual will continue to incur mitigation costs until:

$$(N - N') = E$$

The demand for the mitigation of environmental damage may be seen as a surrogate demand for environmental protection. Clearly, individuals will commit their resources only if their subjective estimate of the benefits is at least as great as the costs. An indirect measure of individual perception of those costs can thus be derived by looking at the amount of resources allocated to avoiding them. However, an individual's willingness to incur costs is constrained by his or her ability to pay. Therefore this approach will only provide a minimum estimate of the benefits received.

The assumptions implicit in this kind of analysis are that:
  (i) accurate data on the costs of the mitigating expenditures are available;
  (ii) there are no secondary benefits associated with the expenditures.
An example of the use of this method can be seen in a case study of environmental quality aspects of upland agricultural projects in Korea (Kim and Dixon, 1986). This study examined alternative soil-management techniques designed to stabilize upland soils and to enhance agricultural

production. The study used information on lowland paddy farmers who were prepared to incur costs for the construction of dikes to divert water, thus preventing waterborne eroded soil from silting up their fields and damaging their crops. The lowland farmers' subjective valuation of the measures taken to prevent upland soil erosion would be at least as great as the cost they incurred to construct the dikes.

Many development projects have effects on the environment which could be valued using this approach. In the Tulunggagung Drainage Project in Indonesia, for example, the preventive-expenditure method could have been used as part of the benefit-cost analysis. It had been proposed to provide drainage facilities for 21,000 hectares of agricultural land for the town of Tulunggagung in order to eliminate flooding and the damage it caused. The cost of damage to household contents in the frequently inundated area was excluded from the original project appraisal because "residents normally have time to take measures to prevent damage to household contents". The true costs to the residents, however, are both those caused by flood damage and those incurred by taking the preventive measures. Therefore the costs voluntarily incurred by the residents could have been used as a minimum estimate of the value they placed on the benefits of flood control, and thereby avoiding this cost.

We could take an urban water supply project as another example. The preventive-expenditure approach would call for the examination of how much people pay to get water from sources other than the city supply, in order not to be exposed to pathogens. In a city like Jakarta, these sources include door-to-door sales, private wells and filtration systems, boiling water and even bottled water. Which method is chosen depends, in part, on individual income and ability to pay, but a realistic picture of the willingness of various groups of consumers to pay for potable water could be built up from a survey of those individual choices. This amount, summed across all residents and appropriately weighted by population and income distribution, may be substantial. Information like this can be very useful in assessing the social benefits of an improved urban water supply.

Other public services like electricity or trash collection can similarly be analyzed. In each case the analyst should examine how the goods and services to be provided by the project are being supplied at present.

Preventive expenditures are common and, if carefully used, can provide useful data. The strength of the approach is that it relies on observable market behavior and is fairly easy to explain to decision-makers. However, in many developing countries the extent of preventive expediture is more commonly constrained by income than by demand.

Choosing a Technique

All the techniques presented in this chapter have fairly wide applicability. The simplest and most powerful is the one which uses changes in productivity; this approach is useful once the effects of a project on the environment and their consequent effects on productivity have been identified. Similarly, the opportunity-cost and preventive-expenditure approaches are quite robust as they rely on actual (or potential) out-of-pocket expenses to determine values.

Cost-effectiveness analysis is a strong approach if used in a sensitive way with realistic goals. Loss-of-earnings, because of some unresolved biological and ethical issues, has more limited use but can be helpful in assessing health-related projects like potable water and sewage disposal.

We cannot prescribe techniques, since the choice is dependent on many factors. However, any of them, used appropriately, should produce results that can be defended and directly incorporated into project analyses.

5 _Potentially applicable techniques_

This chapter presents additional techniques and approaches which have been used to place values on the environmental impacts of development projects. We call these "potentially applicable" either because they need greater care in their use, make more demands on data or on other resources, or because they require stronger assumptions than the more directly operational techniques presented in Chapter 4. This does not mean that these techniques cannot be used; many of them can add to project appraisal by explicitly incorporating the monetary costs of environmental impacts.

The eight techniques presented here (see Table 3) fall into two broad categories: those that use surrogate markets to determine values, and those classified as cost-analysis techniques which assess the magnitude of potential expenditures. The degree to which each technique is directly operational is discussed at the end of the chapter.

Techniques in which Surrogate Market Prices are Used

Many aspects of the environment have no established market price. Things like clean air, unobstructed views, and pleasant surroundings are public goods; therefore direct market prices for them are rarely available. In many cases, however, it is possible to estimate an implicit value for an environmental good or service by means of the price paid for another good which is marketed.

Surrogate-market techniques, therefore, offer approaches which use an actual market price with which to value an unmarketed quality of the environment. The basic assumption is that the price differential, arrived at after all other variables except environmental quality have been controlled for, reflects a purchaser's valuation of the environmental qualities at issue. While there are some limitations to these techniques (to be discussed later), they can, in certain cases, be very useful in valuing a wide range of environmental qualities.

PROPERTY VALUES

In practice property values are a prime example of the surrogate-market approach. The value of a house, for example, is affected by many variables including size, construction, location and the quality of its environment. When the variables of size, construction and location (in terms of proximity to work and shops) are controlled for, much of the price differential between similar units reflects the remaining variables related to environmental quality. A house built by a beach or with a beautiful view is an example. The information gathered from the consequent variations in house price may be used as a surrogate for measuring the unpriced variable.

The basic assumption is that purchasers of property will reveal their attitude to a bundle of attributes (some structural, some environmental, some aesthetic) by their willingness to pay. This is commonly true of residential properties. If no values were placed on environmental or other non-marketed attributes, then one would expect the value of a house to be equal to its construction costs plus an appropriate mark-up. In reality, of course, house prices reflect a very large range of attributes, only some of which are physical. The property-value approach is designed to control for certain variables so that any remaining price differential can then be assigned to the unpriced environmental good. Similarly, environmental "bads" can be measured using this technique, as with a drop in property value due to increased noise or air pollution, or view obstruction.

· As usually applied, the property-value approach needs extensive data on the selling prices of individual units and on a host of physical characteristics. Most of these variables, like the number of rooms, the floor space, construction materials and so forth, are easily measured. But in addition there will be one, unpriced, environmental variable like the levels of noise or air pollution. A multiple regression analysis is then undertaken and a coefficient is estimated for the environmental "bad"; this coefficient is then used to value changes in environmental quality. In another version of the

FIGURE 6: *Willingness to Pay for 1pphm Improvement in NO$_x$ Concentration By NO$_x$ Level for Households at Three Income Levels (log–log version)*

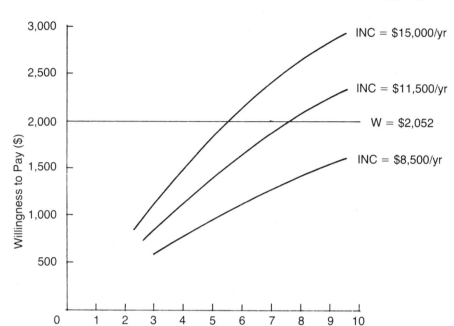

Source: D. Harrison and D.O. Rubinfeld, "Hedonic Housing Prices and the Demand for Clear Air", *Journal of Environmental Economics and Management*, Vol. 5 (1978), pp. 81–102

approach the "priced" variables are controlled for and any residual property value is then assigned to the unpriced environmental good.

The property-value approach is described in some detail in the *Guide* (pp. 195–209) and an example is given based on a study of the effect of air pollution on housing values in Boston (Harrison and Rubinfield, 1978a, 1978b). One result of the study is a graph illustrating the relationship between willingness to pay for a 1pphm improvement in nitrogen oxide (NO$_x$) levels for households at three different income levels (Figure 6). Not surprisingly, households with higher incomes were willing (and able) to pay more for a given improvement in NO$_x$ levels. The curves for all three income groups slope upwards, indicating that households are willing to pay more for a 1pphm improvement the higher the initial level of pollution. That is, the worse the present level of pollution, the more people are willing to pay for a unit reduction in the NO_x level.

Obviously a great number of assumptions and considerable data are needed in order to undertake a property-value study. Some of these assumptions have been criticized by Mäler (1977) and are listed in the *Guide* (p. 207). However, there may well be projects in which the approach could be used. For example, the benefits from an urban project for flood control could, in part, be estimated by examining price differences between housing units located in the flood-prone district and similar housing in less frequently flooded areas. As with any non-market valuation technique, the applications have to be thought out carefully and all assumptions made explicit. While a precise evaluation may not be possible, an order of magnitude of the value placed on the environmental attribute may be obtained.

OTHER LAND-VALUE APPROACHES

Other land-value approaches are based on the same principle as that for property values. Here an observable market price (usually that of retail land prices) is used to evaluate a combination of impacts. If nearby parcels of land are priced differently, for example, any differences between them will normally be due to one of two factors: the productivity of the piece of land or unpriced environmental qualities. The productivity of the land may be evaluated by measuring the change in the value of output described earlier, and the capitalized value of productivity should be reflected in the retail price of land. In addition, there may be other unpriced impacts that are also incorporated in land values. These could include such things as aesthetic values, decreased risks of flooding or of some other environmental catastrophe (although some of these should be captured in the productivity analysis), or increased attractiveness as a habitat for wildlife. By examining land prices and the capitalized value of production from that land, the residual can be determined. Part of this residual represents the "surrogate" value of environmental or other unpriced factors.

Underground transmission lines for utilities provide an example. Domestic electricity, for instance, can be provided by power lines laid either above or below ground. Most people prefer them to be underground, but then they are more costly to install. Are the benefits worth the extra cost? In using the land-value technique the market price of similar parcels of land would be established to see if there was any difference between those with power lines above and those with power lines below ground. If such a difference were to be found, then the amount could be interpreted as representing the capitalized value of the "benefit" from underground power lines.

In sum, the land-value approach uses real market prices for land with varying attributes as a measure for determining the value of an environmental attribute which is not normally priced. It is, of course, essential when using this method to ensure that any differences are net of the value of the direct effects on productivity (although the latter are valid measures of environmental benefits from many soil and water resources management projects).

WAGE DIFFERENTIALS

The technique using wage differentials is similar to that using property values. It rests on the theory that in a perfectly competitive equilibrium, the demand for labor equals the value of the marginal product of the workers and that the supply of labor varies not only with wages, but also with working and living conditions. Thus a higher wage is needed to induce workers to work in polluted areas or to undertake risky occupations. Workers are presumed to be able to move freely among jobs and therefore to be able to choose particular jobs in particular areas at certain wages which will maximize their utility. This approach cannot be used if wages are set centrally unless they are systematically varied to achieve equilibrium in the labor market and unless laborers have freedom of movement.

Difference in wage levels for similar jobs may be viewed as a function of different levels in the attributes of a job relating to working and living conditions. If such a relationship between wage levels and attributes could be estimated, implicit prices (as in the property-value approach) could be determined. Assuming constant implicit prices (reflecting marginal willingness to pay or the acceptance of lower or higher wages for lower or higher levels of the particular attribute), benefits could be estimated for improvements in levels of attributes.

Many attributes which affect wage differentials can be identified. The two of interest and the two to which most examples refer, however, are the risks to life and health and the presence of urban amenities or, especially in the case of air pollution, the lack of them. The implicit price of an urban amenity would provide a trade-off value between air pollution and income.

Few good examples exist for the use of this technique; some are discussed briefly in the *Guide* (pp. 214–15). As far as developing countries are concerned, the use of this approach may be limited by the degree of competitiveness of the labor market, the extent of the flows of information and the degree of labor mobility. Nevertheless, if certain occupations present environmental hazards to the workers and they are to be offered a higher wage in compensation, then the technique can be used to estimate the cost of that hazard or the benefit of eliminating it.

TRAVEL COST

The travel-cost approach has been used extensively in developed countries to value recreational goods and services. Developed in the late 1950s and 1960s (Clawson, 1959; Clawson and Knetsch, 1966) it is based on the simple proposition that observed behavior can be used to derive a demand curve and to estimate a value (including consumer's surplus) for an unpriced environmental good by treating increasing travel costs as a surrogate for variable admission prices.

The transaction price for most goods can be considered to be an expression of willingness to pay for the right to consume the good or the utility received from it. Recreational (or cultural, historic or scenic) goods are, however, a different case. Usually such goods (a public park will be used here as an example) are provided either free of charge or for a nominal admission fee. The value of the benefits or utility derived from a park, however, is often much larger than the fee, with the difference being equal to consumer's surplus. To estimate the total amount of consumer's surplus, we must derive a demand curve from the actual use of the park.

The present pattern of park use is determined by means of a survey. Respondents are questioned about the time and money they spend travelling to the park, distance to the site, and a variety of other socioeconomic variables. The park users' zones of origin are usually defined in terms of increasing distance from, or cost of travel to, the park. A survey will normally show that the frequency with which people use the park (usually measured as a number of visits per thousand of population in each zone) is inversely related to their distance from the site. The more it costs, in time

FIGURE 7: *Plot of Hypothetical Survey Data Used in the Travel-Cost Approach*

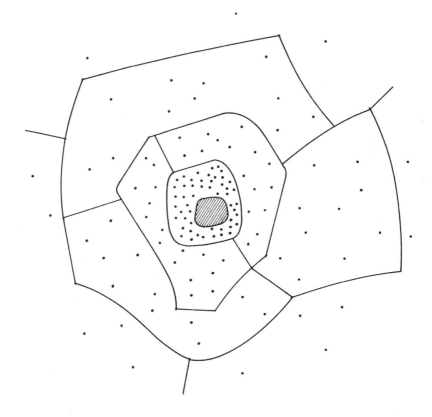

Note: Each dot represents 10 visitors to the park. For each zone a visitation rate (visitors per 1,000 population) is developed.

and money, to get there, the less frequently an individual will use the park, all other factors held equal. If plotted, this information will appear as in Figure 7.

In order to derive the demand curve, a number of assumptions must be made and a number of steps must be taken. The first assumption is that individuals can be grouped into residential zones where the inhabitants have similar preferences. Second, we assume that people will react to increasing travel costs in much the same way as they would react to increased admission charges at the park. This means that at some level of admission fee (or cost of travel) no one would use the park because, given other recreational options, it would be too expensive. Then we make a calculation of visitation rates from all origin zones, taking into account a number of variables related to income, cost of travel and other elements.

In its simplest form a regression equation is derived that relates visitation rates to the cost of travel. This is then used to determine the area of consumer's surplus for park users in each zone. This is calculated zone by zone using the travel-cost equation and the initial values for each particular zone. As the cost of travel from each zone increases the projected visitation rates drop. The objective is to determine consumers' willingness to pay, up to the point at which no one from a given zone would visit the park. In effect, a demand curve for the zone is traced out and the "admission price" at which the demand for the park would equal zero is determined. The area below the calculated demand curve and above the cost curve is used as an estimate of the consumer's surplus of present park users from that zone. This calcu-lation is repeated for each zone and the consumer's surplus from all zones is added together to estimate the total consumer's surplus for users of the park.

It should be stressed that the amount of the travel cost *per se* is not equal to the value of the park. The travel-cost data are used only to estimate a demand curve. Further, the approach uses pre-established patterns of use in order to determine value and is heavily influenced by the existence of other sites. Numerous refinements of the approach are possible and many of these are discussed in considerable detail in the *Guide* (pp. 216–32).

Although this approach would not at first seem applicable to many projects, it can often be used to place a value on a component of a larger project. A dam/reservoir project, for example, may result in the creation of facilities for boating, swimming and sport fishing. The travel-cost techique could be used to place a value on the recreational facilities, but only after the reservoir was in use. (An analysis of a similar reservoir could be done to derive an estimate of recreational benefits *before* the proposed reservoir is built. Obviously this would have to be handled very carefully and all assumptions be made explicit.)

The value of cultural or historical sites threatened by development projects could also be analyzed by the travel-cost method. In such cases the value obtained should be clearly identified as a minimum valuation of only part of the total value of the resource. This point is discussed further in Chapter 7.

MARKETED GOODS AS ENVIRONMENTAL SURROGATES

Sometimes a privately marketed good may be an adequate but imperfect substitute for some environmental service or publicly provided good. For example, private swimming pools may substitute for clean lakes and streams, or private parks for national parks. The potential benefits of an increase in the supply of an environmental good, such as national parks, may be deduced from the demand for the private good. Because the two are close substitutes, the users' level of welfare will not change significantly.

In the case of perfect substitutes, the problem is reduced to the careful specification of the situation and the identification of the changes in use that might be expected. For imperfect substitutes, the value of the new environmental good may be somewhat different from that of the existing private substitute, making the valuation process more difficult.

Some development projects may be valued using this approach. For example, a public water supply system may replace the private distribution and sale of water. It would be possible to examine the cost of privately sold water in order to arrive at the value its consumers place on it. Of course, a municipal system will generally charge a lower cost per unit and so rates of use will also increase. None the less, the approach helps to determine the order of magnitude of potential benefits.

If the enviromental good in question is a recreational resource, the results of this technique can be compared to those from the travel-cost approach. While it is extremely unlikely that the results from both approaches will be identical, there should be a correspondence in the orders of magnitude of the two estimates.

Cost Analysis

Three approaches that may be classified as cost-analysis techniques were presented in Chapter 4. They were the cost-effectiveness, preventive-expenditure and opportunity-cost approaches. All of them were dealt with as "generally applicable" because, by using market prices, they relied on actual expenditures. Here we present cost-analysis techniques which depend on estimates of *potential* expenditures to value a development impact on the environment. Each approach examines the costs that would be involved if some impact on the environment were to be mitigated by replacing the services which had been damaged or destroyed. This information is then used to decide whether it is more efficient to take preventive measures beforehand or compensatory measures after the event.

All three techniques are similar; they are presented separately, however, because there are certain situations in which one will be more appropriate than another.

REPLACEMENT COSTS

The basic premise of the replacement-cost approach is that the costs incurred in replacing productive assets damaged by a project can be measured, and that these costs can be interpreted as an estimate of the benefits presumed to flow from measures taken to prevent that damage from occurring. The rationale for this technique is similar to that for preventive expenditures except that the replacement costs are not a subjective valuation of the potential damages but, rather, are the true costs of replacement if damage has actually occurred. The approach may thus be interpreted as an "accounting procedure" used to work out whether it is more efficient to let damage happen and then to repair it or to prevent it from happening in the first place. It gives an estimate of the upper limit but does not really measure the benefits of environmental protection *per se*.

The assumptions implicit in this type of analysis are:
  (i) the magnitude of damage is measurable;
  (ii) the replacement costs are calculable and are not greater than the value of the productive resources destroyed; and therefore it is economically efficient to make the replacement. If this assumption is not true, it would not make sense to replace the resource lost; and
  (iii) there are no secondary benefits associated with the expenditures.
An example of the use of this approach may be seen in the case study by Kim and Dixon (1986), which examined the viability of alternative soil-stabilization techniques in upland agricultural areas in Korea. The damaged productive asset was the upland soil. The cost of physically replacing lost soil and nutrients was taken as a measure of the potential benefits of preventing soil erosion and nutrient loss. The implicit assumption (which may be a strong one) is that the erosion is worth preventing: that is, that the productive value of the soil is greater than the cost of replacement. In this case the costs of the proposed steps to prevent the erosion of the

soil were lower than those of replacement, so the preventive measures were thought to be economically justifiable.

A forestry development project in Luzon, Philippines, is an example of a project where replacement-cost techniques could have been used. It involved the establishment of 10,700 hectares of tree plantations, measures to protect vegetation from fire and uncontrolled grazing on a further 1,300 hectares which are too steep for planting trees, and the development of pasture land, cut-and-carry fodder supply land, and agroforestry on a further 1,000 hectares.

The only benefit quantified in the project appraisal was that of wood production for various purposes. The slowing of severe soil erosion with a resultant reduction in the siltation of reservoirs, rivers and irrigation canals, the decreased incidence of flooding, were all regarded as non-quantifiable benefits. Much as in the Korean case cited above, the cost of replacing the lost soil and nutrients could have been used as the basis on which to estimate the value of the benefits from the reduction in soil erosion. In this case the decrease in soil erosion was a secondary benefit of the project, so the information derived from the replacement cost would not be used to evaluate the direct project costs but would be included as a benefit.

Both the Korean and Philippine examples could also be evaluated using a productivity approach, either to examine the potential loss in production if no replacement is carried out, or to estimate the value of present production. In either case the information obtained can be used to assess whether or not replacement is economically justified.

In general, the replacement-cost approach can be useful when an effect on the environment has caused, or will cause, money to be spent on replacing a physical asset. When that asset is a road, dam or bridge, the technique is straightforward. When it is soil, water or aquatic life, its application is the same but the problems of measurement are greater. The change-in-productivity approach can also be useful in these cases. When impacts on the environment result in physical economic externalities, then this approach can frequently be used to bring those externalities into the analysis.

RELOCATION COSTS

This is a variant of the replacement-cost technique. In it, the actual costs of relocating a physical facility because of changes in the quality of the environment are used to evaluate the potential benefits (and associated costs) of preventing the environmental change. For example, the construction of an oil palm mill would result in the discharge of waste water into a nearby stream. Of the various environmental costs associated with this discharge, one might be the need to relocate an intake for a domestic water supply which is, at present, downstream from the mill. If additional waste water treatment equipment is installed in the downstream water intake rather than relocating the intake, then the equipment costs become an example of preventive expenditure.

SHADOW PROJECTS

In an attempt to estimate the cost of replacing the entire range of environmental goods and services threatened by a project, the shadow-project technique was developed.

This is a special type of replacement-cost technique. If environmental services, the benefits of which are difficult to value, will be lost or diminished as a result of a development project, then their economic costs can be approximated by examining the costs of a hypothetical supplementary project which would provide substitutes. Take, for example, a project which requires harvesting a significant part of a mangrove forest. An alternative investment could be conceived which would, in principle, provide the same output of goods and services as does the mangrove forest. The total cost of the alternative can then be added to the basic resource cost of the project in order to estimate its full cost. It should be noted that the supplementary or "shadow" project need only be conceptual and not actually built in order to arrive at an estimate of its costs. Inclusion of shadow-project costs gives some indication of how great the benefits of the new project must be in order to outweigh the losses it causes.

The assumptions implicit in this type of analysis are:
  (i) the endangered resource is scarce and highly valued;
  (ii) the human-built alternative would provide the same quantity and quality of goods and services as does the natural environment;
  (iii) the original level of goods and services is desirable and should therefore be maintained;
  (iv) the costs of the shadow project do not exceed the value of the lost productive service of the natural environment.

In general, shadow-project analysis is used to give an estimate of the order of magnitude of the cost of replacing a threatened environmental good or service. It may frequently be that recognition of the enormous cost, or even the impossibility, of replacing an environmental resource (a beach, a lake, a river, a tropical forest) will lead to greater concern about preventing the loss in the first place.

SUMMARY

Cost-side approaches are frequently very useful because they involve tangible actions which have directly observable market prices. Both the replacement-cost and the relocation-cost techniques (and the associated shadow-project approach) are examples of ways of establishing the costs of measures to be taken to mitigate negative impacts on the environment. If the replaced or relocated environmental good or service is a perfect substitute for the damaged resource, then these techniques give an upper estimate of the economic cost of the damage. That is, if the cost of preventing the damage is less than the cost either of replacement or of relocation, then it is economically worthwhile to take that course (assuming that benefits of preventing the damage are greater than the costs). On the other hand, if the replacement or relocation costs do not completely compensate for the environmental damage, then they do not establish a true upper limit to the cost estimates.

Take as an example a stream that is used for both fish production and as an urban water supply. If a factory is built and that stream, as a consequence, becomes so polluted by waste that the water plant must be relocated, the cost of that relocation is not the upper boundary of the "cost" of the factory pollution. The lost fish production and the loss of other, perhaps unpriced, goods and services should also be included.

Choosing a Technique

Even though this chapter is about "potentially applicable" techniques, the approaches described here deserve serious consideration when evaluating the environmental impacts of projects. If one of the generally applicable techniques presented in Chapter 4 cannot, for some reason, be used, then the "menu" of techniques given here may well provide a useful alternative.

Perhaps the most directly useful techniques given in this chapter are the various cost-analysis approaches. Since they use market prices and rely on actual or potential expenditures, measurement problems are minimized. Relocation costs, for example, are a direct way of evaluating the benefits and costs of prevention or of mitigation.

Surrogate-market-based techniques are also useful but, because they use indirect measures of value, have to be interpreted cautiously. None the less, in those countries which have well-developed property markets, the techniques using property or land values may be used. The travel-cost approach is widely used in the West and, in theory, could be used in certain developing countries.

6 *Additional methods of valuing environmental impacts*

Two distinct classes of techniques are presented in this chapter. The first class, contingent valuation methods, is a group of survey-based methods which may be used to value the environmental impacts of development projects in the absence of data on market or surrogate-market prices. Macroeconomic models, the other class, may be used to examine the interaction between the environment and large-scale economic growth. Although these techniques may not be immediately usable in the analysis of many projects in developing countries, they are presented here because they are valuable tools in some cases. For example, macroeconomic models could be used by national planners as aids to their understanding of the environmental problems likely to arise as a result of economic growth.

Contingent Valuation Methods

In some cases, where data are unavailable or where there are no alternative markets, it may not be possible to value the environmental effects of a particular project by using the market or surrogate-market methods set out in Chapters 4 and 5. These cases include such diverse goods and services as species preservation, historical or cultural phenomena, genetic diversity and preservation of open spaces, unobstructed views or public access to amenity resources. A viable alternative here may be the use of the contingent valuation methods (CVM), sometimes also referred to as hypothetical valuation.

These techniques involve the direct questioning of consumers to determine how they would react to certain situations. Unlike market and surrogate-market techniques, estimates are not based on observed behavior but, instead, by inferring what an individual's behavior would be from the answers he or she provides in a survey framework. This approach can be useful in evaluating components of development projects which cannot be measured using other methods. Although they may not always yield precise estimates, they do provide an order-of-magnitude estimate which can be very valuable. An overview of survey-based valuation techniques is found in the *Guide* (pp. 232–54) and a comprehensive assessment is presented in Cummings, Brookshire and Schulze (1986).

Most of the techniques set out in Chapters 4 and 5 examine changes in the quality of the environment in aggregated form and then place a value on the change. In contrast, the CVM techniques start with the individual and his or her perception of change. Once values for a representative set of people have been determined, they are aggregated to a total value directly dependent on the number of individuals affected.

CVM techniques rely on standard neoclassical economic principles and use either of two Hicksian measures of consumer's surplus: compensating variation (CV) or equivalent variation (EV). Compensating variation is the amount of payment or change in income necessary to make an individual indifferent between an initial situation and a new situation with different prices. Equivalent variation may be viewed as a change in income equal to a gain in welfare resulting from a change in price. Alternatively, it may be considered as the minimum payment needed to persuade an individual voluntarily to forgo a price decrease. In the case of a price increase, EV is the maximum amount an individual will pay to avoid that increase. The difference between the two measures is that CV uses the initial level of utility as a reference point while EV evaluates the change from the *ex-post hoc* level of utility. Ordinary Marshallian consumer's surplus is sometimes used as an estimate of the more technically correct CV and EV. Freeman (1979) discusses the various consumer's surplus measures in depth.

A description follows of the various contingent valuation methods in current use and the problems associated with them.

BIDDING GAMES

There are different varieties of bidding game, though they have certain features in common. In a bidding game, each individual is asked to evaluate a hypothetical situation and to express his or her willingness to pay (WTP) for, or willingness to accept compensation (WTAC) for, a certain change in the level of provision of a good. This technique is most often used to value public goods like access to parks, clean air or water or unobstructed views.

The essential feature of public goods is that one person's consumption does not affect the amount available to the next person (although some public goods, such as recreational areas, may be subject to congestion beyond a certain point). Clean air or public defense are classic examples of public goods. Once provided, the marginal cost of an additional person using a public good is zero. Therefore, all respondents' willingness to pay rather than to do without the good may be summed to provide an estimate of aggregate willingness to pay. In economic terms this is analogous to the vertical summation of individual compensated demand curves.

There are two major types of bidding games: single bid games and iterative (or converging) bid games. In the former an interviewer, after describing a good (for example, preservation of an endangered species, or a certain improvement in air quality) to a respondent, asks him or her to name the maximum price they would be willing to pay for the good or to name the minimum level of compensation they would accept in exchange for losing the option to purchase that good. The responses are then averaged and extrapolated to arrive at an aggregate willingness to pay or an aggregate level of compensation for the population as a whole.

In iterative bidding games the respondent, rather than being asked to name a sum, is asked whether he should or would pay $X for the situation or good described. This amount is then varied iteratively until a maximum willingness to pay (or a minimum willingness to accept compensation) is reached.

Although both types of bidding game may be useful, survey practitioners are split over their relative merits. One objection to the iterative technique is the potential existence of "starting-point bias". This is the idea that the interviewer may bias the respondent's answer by establishing a reference point for an acceptable range of bids. Another disadvantage is that although single bid games can be conducted either in person or through a mail survey, iterative bidding games can take place only in face-to-face interviews. One advantage of iterative bidding games is that answers often have a lower standard deviation around the mean as compared with single bid games.

"Hypothetical bias" is another problem inherent in bidding games and in survey techniques in general. People may not give answers which reflect their true values, particularly if they have no incentive to answer correctly questions which take time and thought. Another source of bias may be if people try to act strategically. This "strategic bias" will reflect what respondents feel will be done with their answers. If they feel they may actually have to pay the amount they answer, they may undervalue their true response. If they feel that high answers will bring about changes they would like to see but they know they will not actually have to pay this amount, they may overstate the amount they would actually be willing to pay.

Bidding games and possible biases are discussed in detail in Rowe and Chestnut (1982). Although their discussion focuses on the valuation of visibility benefits, much of the information is applicable to valuation of other environmental goods and services.

These problems notwithstanding, surveys can be of great value in estimating economic values for effects which cannot otherwise be easily measured. Carefully worded surveys, properly conducted, can provide a great deal of information from those people who will actually be affected by a proposed project.

TAKE-IT-OR-LEAVE-IT EXPERIMENTS

In a take-it-or-leave-it experiment, respondents are randomly divided into sub-samples or cells. Each sub-sample is then asked the same question, but each is offered a different amount of money and is asked either to take it or leave it. For example, an experiment attempting to find out people's willingness to accept a decrease in air quality might ask different groups of respondents if they would be willing to accept $10, $20, or $50 to allow the air in their neighborhood to become more polluted. Each person is given only one amount to respond to, and the various amounts are randomly distributed over the entire surveyed population. The end result is a number of cells each with a certain proportion of people who would or who would not accept the payment offered. These answers can then be analyzed using a logit model which will yield a willingness to pay for the average consumer. The aggregate willingness to pay can then be arrived at by multiplying this level by the number of people affected.

One advantage of this technique is that it more closely simulates an actual market. Respondents are offered something at a given price and can then decide whether or not to "purchase" it.

TRADE-OFF GAMES

In trade-off games participants must choose between different bundles of goods. What is offered will, most often, be a mix of money and differing levels, or quantities, of an environmental good. The respondent is given a situation with a base level of an environmental good provided. Next she or he is offered an alternative in which the environmental good is increased, but at a price. The respondent may then choose between these. The price of the increase is then varied until the respondent sees no advantage in one alternative over the other.

For example, in a situation attempting to determine willingness to pay for a larger neighborhood park, the choices might be to pay no money and keep the original park or to pay a certain amount and get a five-hectare addition. The question would be repeated with different amounts of money until the point is found where the respondent is indifferent between paying no money and keeping the original park or paying a certain amount of money and receiving the park addition. The result may then be interpreted as the marginal compensated demand price for the environmental good. (See the *Guide* for an application of this technique.)

COSTLESS CHOICE

Costless choice involves offering participants two or more alternatives, each of which is desirable and will cost nothing, and then questioning them directly to determine which they would prefer. One example might involve a choice between a certain sum of money or some unpriced environmental good (a reduction in air or noise pollution, or improved availability of public recreation facilities). If the individual chooses the environmental good rather than the money, then that would establish the minimum value of the environmental good to that individual. If the money were chosen rather than the good, then it would be established that the individual thought the good to be worth less than the sum of money.

Another version of this technique is to offer the respondent the choice between several well-known goods with established but differing values, and an unpriced environmental good. In a developed country, such goods might be a soft drink, a movie ticket, a dinner for two at a fine restaurant as compared with the opportunity to spend a day at a nearby lake. By calculating the value of those well-known goods which the respondent would reject in favor of the environmental good, it is possible to establish a range of values for the latter. Care must be taken to ensure that the goods are familiar and of approximately the same value to all respondents.

Costless choice may be useful in a developing country where actual market prices are not well established and few things are exchanged for money. In this situation, choices might include a kilo of rice, a day's worth of firewood, or other commonly traded goods. Such an approach may be more realistic to the respondent than the more abstract bidding game approach.

DELPHI TECHNIQUE

Delphi techniques differ from the survey techniques described so far in that "experts" rather than consumers are questioned. These experts, by an iterative process, try to place a value on a particular good. The Delphi technique has been used to place values on a diverse set of resources including the preservation values for endangered species, allocation of limited budgets across competing areas, determination of minimum habitat size for preservation of genetic diversity, and the appropriate mix between development and conservation.

The technique involves asking each of a group of experts to value or price a particular good. The values chosen are then circulated with that member's explanation for his/her choice. After seeing these opinions, the experts are then asked to reconsider their estimates and to come to a new decision. Ideally, each successive round should bring the values closer together until they cluster tightly around a mean value.

Normally members of such a group are not assembled, or, if they are, then the individual estimates are communicated in writing and not orally. This prevents direct confrontation between the experts and helps to prevent any one person from dominating the group. The results of the Delphi process will depend on the quality of the experts involved, their ability to reflect societal values and the manner in which the process is undertaken.

THE LIMITATIONS OF CONTINGENT VALUATION

Because the contingent valuation methods do not analyze actual behavior, the most important question concerns their accuracy in simulating the conditions of the real world. Surveys are, by their nature, hypothetical and, furthermore, people have little experience in making explicit decisions about the value of environmental goods.

Survey techniques are subject to a number of biases, including those described in the section on bidding games. In addition to those previously described, other biases may affect the reliability of the results.

An *information bias* can arise either as a result of providing too little information about the choices offered or from misleading statements by the interviewer. Ideally, survey respondents should be provided with clear, complete and unbiased specifications for the choices.

In some types of survey, an *instrument bias* can arise if the respondent is hostile to the means by which payment would be collected. The vehicle chosen for payment – various forms of taxation, entrance fee or user fee – may result in different willingness-to-pay responses. Moreover, some people accustomed to certain public goods being provided free of charge may protest at any kind of payment and be unwilling to pay anything. Adding an additional question to make sure that any zero bid from the respondent actually reflects zero value to them, rather than a "protest" against payment, can often eliminate this kind of bias.

One last problem is how to decide whether compensating variation or equivalent variation is the most appropriate measure of consumer's surplus. In theory, in most cases they should provide similar estimates, differing only in the effect on income caused by whether payment is made or received, and by the fact that willingness to pay is constrained by income. In practice, however, estimates obtained by using willingness to accept compensation as a measure are often much larger than those obtained from using willingness to pay (see Knetsch and Sinden, 1984, for an interesting example of this phenomenon).

The appropriate measure largely depends on property rights. Willingness to pay would be the correct measure if the right at issue is vested in the polluters, whereas willingness to accept compensation may be the preferred alternative if consumers have the "property right" of a clean environment.

Properly planned and conducted surveys can, however, eliminate most of these problems. Since the costs of surveys increase with the number of people surveyed, the decision about their size must weigh the benefits of greater accuracy from larger samples against the additional costs. Care must also be taken that the sampling technique is statistically valid.

The level of accuracy is also affected by the way in which the hypothetical situation is described to the respondent. This should be as specific as possible and the alternative should be equally clearly outlined. The clearer the hypothetical situation, the less the effort called for from the respondent. Since in most cases little incentive is offered for an accurate answer, enough information must be given to allow the respondents to visualize the alternatives without undue effort.

Despite limitations, the methods of contingent valuation may, at times, be the best way to measure the effects of changes to the environment on social welfare. They may also be helpful in validating estimates of consumer's surplus obtained by more conventional methods.

Macroeconomic Models

Development projects often affect environmental quality and resource sustainability on a regional level, not only on or around the project site. Under such circumstances the measurement of benefits and costs needs to be considered within broader boundaries. For this purpose, general-equilibrium and systems-analysis models can help to overcome the problems involved in accounting for secondary economic and environmental effects.

GENERALIZED INPUT-OUTPUT MODELS

Generalized input-output (I-O) analysis is one of the many ways of including the repercussions of development activity on the economy and on the environment in an analysis.

Developed by Leontief in the late 1930s, I-O analysis is based on the interrelationships of production activities in modern economic systems. Each producing activity acts in two ways. First, it supplies its output to other industries and to final buyers. Second, it buys inputs: the products of other industries, labor skills, capital services, natural resources, land, managerial expertise and imported materials. The value of output is made up of the value of materials and services purchased from other sectors plus the value of primary inputs used directly in the production process. The final demands for economic goods and services act as the driving force for the whole system.

Input-output analysis consists of tables which describe, for a number of sectors within the economic system, the inputs to the processes of production during a certain period along with the outputs realized as a result. The input and output flows are usually measured in monetary units.

In order to include environmental concerns in this framework, several parts are added to the basic tables describing the emissions of different types of environmental pollution caused by the different sectors in the economic system. Those sectors which exist solely for the abatement of pollution are also described. These discharges of residuals and demands for inputs from the environment are handled in a fashion similar to primary inputs such as capital and labor, and are again driven by final demand for economic goods and services.

By changing final demand patterns and structural relationships in the model, different options for economic development, residuals discharges and ambient environmental quality can be generated. This will assist policy-makers in choosing what they consider to be the best development plan.

While the actual construction of an input-output model will not be discussed here, the general format of an extended I-O model incorporating environmental concerns is illustrated in Figure 8. The elements of a traditional I-O model are shown by the shaded boxes: the matrix of direct requirement coefficients, A_{11}, the matrix of primary inputs, V_1, and the matrix of final demands, F. The unshaded boxes model the production of pollutants and inputs for pollution-abatement activities. More details on the construction of an I-O model and its application to an environmental management problem are found in the *Guide*, pp. 287–300.

LIMITATIONS OF INPUT-OUTPUT MODELS

Although the extension of an I-O analysis to environmental phenomena seems to be straightforward, it leaves several problems unsolved. Some of these are due to inherent problems of input-output models and some to the manner in which repercussions on the environment are modeled. These problems include:

(i) Utilizing the input-output model as a production function in an economic model means that strong assumptions are made on the linearity of production processes: that is, input coefficients are treated as fixed.

FIGURE 8: *Input–Output Tables, including Environmental Pollution and Pollution Abatement*

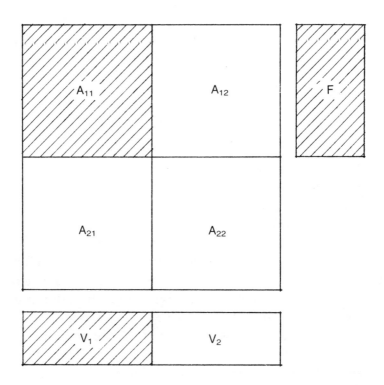

Notes: A_{11} = matrix of intermediary deliveries between traditional economic sectors.

A_{21} = matrix of emissions of several types of pollutants caused by the activities of the existing sectors in the economic system.

A_{12} = matrix of inputs from existing economic sectors in pollution abatement sectors.

A_{22} = matrix of emissions of several types of pollutants caused by the abatement sectors.

V_1 = matrix of primary inputs in traditional economic sectors.

V_2 = matrix of primary inputs and imports for abatement sectors.

F = matrix of final deliveries by traditional economic sectors to consumers, government, firms and exports.

Source: D.E. James, H.M.A. Jansen and J.B. Opschoor, *Economic Approaches to Environmental Problems* (Amsterdam: Elsevier Scientific, 1978).

(ii) As a result, substitution between inputs resulting from pollution abatement is easily neglected.

(iii) The effects of international competition between national industries are not taken into account.

(iv) Little attention is given to other means of reducing the emission of pollutants. For instance, when the importance of environmental conservation is acknowledged, new capital goods may have a quite different technical profile from existing capital stock. This may include the more efficient use of other raw materials and the recycling of waste products.

(v) Even though pollution problems are conceptually dealt with in distinct sectors, the fact is that pollution is often treated by use of end-of-line equipment installed by the polluting company.

These limitations on the use of input-output analysis have led to important adaptations. Methods have been developed to adapt I-O coefficients to changing technological circumstances – for example, Linear Programming and its extended methods, and Quadratic/Least Squares methods.

Another major drawback is the amount of time and effort involved in collecting the basic data. It is unlikely that many developing countries possess national input-output tables with data on environmental quality. To construct even a modest input-output model requires several years of work and a great deal of cooperation from government and industry. There is a risk that by the time the data have been compiled, the model for making accurate policy appraisals will already be outdated. Finally, even though the "best" strategy can, in principle, be found by iterative procedures, the process can become cumbersome and frustrating for decision-makers, especially when large numbers of variable and diverse opinions are involved.

LINEAR PROGRAMMING MODELS

The preceding section has stressed the importance of using a general-equilibrium model to account for the quality of the environment, both regionally and nationally. However, in complex situations which involve many choices and a large number of variables, mathematical programming models may provide more suitable approaches. Linear programming and its extended models are mathematical programming techniques that have been widely applied to models for the optimization of environmental quality.

Linear programming is primarily concerned with the allocation of scarce resources. The model's purpose is to optimize a predetermined objective, or set of objectives, subject to a set of constraints or to other minor objectives. Decision-makers must specify in advance what weights must be attached to the variables and the implicit properties of the general linear programming model require that the functional relationships in the problem be linear and additive, divisible and deterministic.

When linear programming is applied to account for environmental problems, this is usually done by maximizing the economic benefits of production while at the same time preserving or enhancing environmental quality or minimizing the regional incremental capital cost of controlling emissions. The dual-primal property of every linear programming problem is one of its most useful features because it yields shadow prices for the constraints in the primal problem. The calculated values of shadow prices are especially important for sensitivity analysis.

A shadow price on a constraint indicates how much the value of the objective function changes if the constraint is altered by one unit. Shadow prices are obtained from the dual problem and allow policy-makers to see which particular constraints are exerting the greatest restriction on the attainment of primary objectives. This is particularly relevant to the management and planning of environmental quality, because shadow prices often take the place of actual market prices as guides to the evaluation of unpriced environmental services.

Environmental quality effects can be incorporated into linear programming models in several ways, depending on the nature of the objectives in environmental management, the technologies available for the reduction of pollution and the incentives offered for implementation. Where economically feasible technologies for control are unavailable, effects on the quality of the environment can be regulated by "structural" methods. If economically feasible alternative technologies are available, then "technical" means of reducing pollution can be implemented. For examples of the use of linear programming to address environmental concerns see the *Guide*, pp. 300–18.

LIMITATIONS OF LINEAR PROGRAMMING

Applying linear programming to environmental issues is not an easy task. Inherent problems of linear programming such as the difficulty of incorporating joint costs and economies of scale make it difficult to model realistic situations accurately. The need to assign relative weights to economic and environmental quality may present difficulties to planners and decision-makers.

The solution to linear programming problems is affected by the constraints, since the number of variables in the problem cannot exceed the number of constraints. Insufficient basic constraints lead to oversimplicity, but the incorporation of further, arbitrary, constraints might invalidate the true restrictions on the attainment of planning objectives. Shadow prices in the dual can also be affected by this difficulty and can, therefore, lead to serious mistakes in interpretation.

Finally, like most general-equilibrium models, the technique requires much data gathering, information processing, and computing effort. The planner must take care in deciding whether or not the problem is complex enough to warrant such an elaborate model.

7 *The limits to economic measurement of environmental impacts*

The approaches and techniques described in the preceding chapters are designed to help those planning projects to identify, quantify, monetize and include the environmental effects of the projects they are planning. Some of these techniques are easily applied, while others demand more in the way of data and time. Although the approaches and techniques advocated here are theoretically well founded, there are limitations to the economic measurement of sustainability and environmental effects in general, and specifically to the use of benefit-cost analysis (BCA) for this purpose.

Some of the issues, such as valuing the loss of a human life, are controversial and raise important ethical questions. Others, such as the value of genetic diversity or cultural significance, raise intractable questions of measurement. We will briefly discuss some of these issues, with short descriptions of the relevant questions and thinking concerning them.

Income Distribution

Evaluating economic efficiency is the primary objective of most project analyses, but most governments and development banks are also interested in the effect of projects on income distribution. Traditional economic analysis accepts – or at least does not question – either existing income distribution or that which would prevail following the implementation of an "efficient" project. On the assumptions that underlie BCA, a society will be economically efficient in its use of resources when net monetary social benefits – that is the difference between total monetary benefits and total monetary costs, measured in socially desirable prices – are maximized.

Efficiency is measured without regard to whom the benefits and costs accrue and irrespective of whether society considers the prevailing distribution of income to be desirable. If income distribution is of concern, as it is in most developing countries, then the distribution of costs and benefits must be considered in the BCA. Projects which will primarily benefit already wealthy individuals at the expense of poorer individuals may be undesirable on distributional grounds, even if they show high benefit/cost ratios.

Three different approaches are commonly used to address distributional effects in a project analysis: qualitative consideration, weighting, or the establishment of distributional constraints. In each of these approaches, the analyst's main task is simply to present the information to the decision-maker. It is then up to the decision-maker to determine how to use this information.

The simplest method of providing such information to decision-makers is to estimate net benefits by income class, group or region as applicable. Similarly, adverse impacts of the project and costs of financing must be examined to determine on which groups these burdens will fall. All this information is provided to the decision-maker, who can then evaluate the distributional implications of the project and decide whether the project is acceptable on distributional grounds.

Another alternative is to take the distributional analysis a step further and to assign weights to the benefits received and costs borne by various groups or income classes. Normally, benefits received, or costs borne, by disadvantaged groups are given relatively more weight than those which accrue to wealthier groups. The assignment of weights is clearly a subjective decision and is the job of the decision-maker, not the project analyst. Different schemes of weighting are discussed in Ray (1984), Squire and Van der Tak (1975), and Helmers (1979).

A third approach is to set constraints on the allowable distribution of benefits among different groups. For example, targets can be established which set a minimum acceptable distribution of benefits to a designated low-income class or group. Only those projects in which at least a certain percentage of benefits accrue to that group will be given further consideration. Although the targets must be set by decision-makers, analysts may be asked how to modify projects so that their distributional aspects are improved.

Intergenerational Equity

In addition to affecting income distribution (which can be viewed as intragenerational equity), development projects also affect the inter-generational endowments of resources. The primary objective of "development" is to increase the quality of life by increasing incomes, improving health and nutrition, or in some manner making life easier for those affected by the project. However, the impacts of many projects will be felt for long periods of time, and not all future impacts will be positive.

Consider a development project which replaces a tropical rainforest with grazing land for cattle. While it may be true that the tangible outputs of the rainforest are relatively small compared to the value of the cattle, there are many factors to consider. In many areas, cattle ranching will remain profitable only for a short period – the limited fertility of many altered rainforest lands will support cattle for only a few years before yields begin to decline. Often the end result is degraded, bare land which will support very little in the future. In addition, the many unpriced benefits of the rainforest are lost for ever.

On the other hand, consider a rural forestry development project in a currently degraded area. The area, which may be unused or produce little, may have the potential to support a renewable source of fuelwood and other wood products indefinitely. However, a large amount of investment may be necessary, with no returns to be received for a number of years.

Both of these projects have important implications for future residents of the areas affected. In the former case (cattle grazing), future generations may have fewer resources available to them than they would have had without the project while in the latter (forestry development), both current and future generations may be enriched by the project. Even so, it is quite possible that benefit-cost analyses of the two projects may show the former to be more profitable than the latter. A great deal will depend on the discount rate used in the analysis.

As discussed in Chapter 3, discounting is used to compare costs and benefits which occur at different points in time. The choice of the discount rate to be used will greatly affect the outcome of the analysis. A high discount rate will favor projects with immediate net benefits over those whose benefits will not be realized for a longer period. In addition, the higher the discount rate, the less the influence of negative impacts that may arise in the future. Low discount rates, on the other hand, have less restrictive effects on projects with long-term net benefits and give more weight to negative future impacts.

In effect, discounting results in less and less attention given to successive generations. To eliminate this bias of putting the welfare of the current generation above that of future generations, some people have advocated the use of a very low, or even a zero discount rate. Such suggestions, however, are ill conceived and would not result in efficient, or even equitable use of resources. Clearly, eliminating discounting would violate two essential facts. First, people would rather be given a certain amount of money today than the same amount of money sometime in the future. Second, alternative opportunities exist in which sums of money invested today will yield larger sums of money in the future. For both these reasons, eliminating discounting would result in a net decrease, not an increase, of social welfare.

It is true that both the choice of project selected and the discount rate to be used will affect the intertemporal allocation of resources and thus have implications for intergenerational equity. However, by wisely using non-renewable resources and emphasizing projects which promote sustainable use of renewable resources, the welfare of both current and future generations can be enhanced.

A related issue concerns projects which will have irreversible effects of various kinds. These projects will also have important effects on future generations and are discussed separately later in this chapter.

Risk and Uncertainty

There are a number of ways in which risk and uncertainty enter into project analyses. In a production-oriented development project, future prices and expected yields will be subject to uncertainty. For soil-conservation projects, both the with-project and without-project rates of erosion and/or their effects on productivity may be unknown. Natural events such as drought, windstorms, hail, and plant and animal diseases may seriously affect projects.

All projects face some degree of uncertainty. The most common way of dealing with this is to use "expected values" for prices, quantities and other variables whose precise values cannot be known in advance. Essentially, this involves transforming uncertainty (where the probabilities of different outcomes are not known) into risk (where the probabilities of various outcomes are weighted according to their likelihood of occurrence). Each potential outcome is weighted by the probability of its occurrence, and the weighted outcomes are then summed to arrive at a mean, or expected, value. These probabilities may be estimated by using past trends, subjective judgements or through a variety of advanced techniques (see Pouliquen, 1970).

For example, consider a forestry project where there is some uncertainty about the yield of the project. The following might be the best estimates of annual yields available from the forester:

.4 tons/hectare	20% probability
.5 tons/hectare	40% probability
.6 tons/hectare	30% probability
.7 tons/hectare	10% probability

The expected value of the annual production would be $(.4 \times .2) + (.5 \times .4) + (.6 \times .3) + (.7 \times .1) = .53$ tons/hectare.

This "expected-value" method of accounting for risk and uncertainty is the standard method of incorporating these variables into BCA. One problem with this technique is that it results in the use of a single number which does not indicate the degree of uncertainty or the range of values which might actually be expected. It also does not account for an individual's perception of risk (see Graham, 1981, for a discussion of this topic).

Another means of dealing with risk and uncertainty is the use of *sensitivity analysis*. In sensitivity analysis, the project analysis is modified to examine the effects of different assumptions about key variables, and their effect on the project's overall profitability. Using optimistic and pessimistic values for different variables can indicate which variables will have the most pronounced effects on benefits and costs. Although this does not indicate a probability of occurrence of the upper or lower values, it is a valuable tool in determining which variables are most crucial to the project's success.

Handling risk and uncertainty is a difficult but necessary task in project analysis. For additional information, see Arrow and Lind (1970), Pouliquen (1970), Pearce and Nash (1981), and Haimes (1981).

Irreversibility

Many projects entail the modification of natural habitats. Development of a major project such as a dam, a mine or an industrial facility will preclude other uses of the areas in which they are built. Since these natural lands cannot be replaced at reasonable cost, each project sited in such an area will reduce the supply of these available natural areas. In this sense, the effects of the project are irreversible. The habitat alterations may also endanger the continued existence of plants or animal species – another effect with irreversible consequences.

Projects which may have irreversible impacts must be given special attention. It is impossible accurately to foresee the future, and irreversible impacts which seem unimportant today may ultimately be of considerable importance. This uncertainty about the future implications of today's decisions mandates that extra care be taken to ensure correct decisions.

Some economists view an irreversible action as one which limits future options (Henry, 1974). Others view irreversible results as a constraint in that they limit the range of actions which can be taken subsequently (Miller and Lad, 1984). In this manner, irreversible decisions made today may reduce social welfare in the future since all future choices will be constrained by past decisions which cannot be changed.

One aspect of the value of retaining future options has been referred to as "option value". Krutilla and Fisher (1985) describe option value as "the value, in addition to consumer's surplus, that arises from retaining an option to a good or service for which future demand is uncertain". This can also be viewed as a "risk premium", an amount people would be willing to pay to avoid the risk of not having something available which they may want in the future, over and above its expected value to them. Estimating option value is not an easy task; most attempts involve some form of contingent valuation (see Chapter 6).

Another concept related to irreversibility and uncertainty is referred to as "quasi-option value". This value represents the benefits of delaying a decision when one of the alternatives involves an irreversible choice and uncertainty exists about the benefits of the alternatives. Quasi-option value may be viewed as the expected value of information which could be gained by delaying a decision (Conrad, 1980). It will be positive in most cases since delaying a decision will usually reduce the uncertainty of future values, but it can also be negative if development itself leads to better information for future decisions (Miller and Lad, 1984).

There is no single method for accounting for irreversibility in an economic analysis. The opportunity-cost approach outlined in Chapter 4 is one possibility, since it indirectly provides information on the cost of preservation. In general, if the costs of retaining an option that would otherwise be foreclosed are relatively low, the decision-maker should weigh the possibility of retention carefully.

Another possibility is the use of the Safe Minimum Standard (SMS) criterion (Ciriacy-Wantrup, 1968). This is appropriate when dealing with resources which are renewable up to a point but are subject to irreversible damage. These include soil resources as well as genetic resources such as plants and animals, commonly referred to as biodiversity. Applying the SMS criterion involves calculating a margin of safety to prevent irreversible damage to the resource. If such a standard can be maintained without "excessive" costs, the resource should be protected. It is up to the policy-maker, of course, to decide at what level costs become "excessive".

The question of biodiversity – its current state and policy options – is receiving increased global attention. Wilson (1988) presents a comprehensive overview of current thinking on biodiversity issues.

Value of Human Life

Chapter 4 outlined methods of evaluating projects which will affect human health. However, projects which will directly save or, alternatively, take lives cannot be evaluated in the same manner, since the ethical considerations involved transcend economic analysis. For more detailed considerations of this topic, see the references given in Chapter 4.

Incrementalism

Incrementalism is the term used to denote problems which arise from making decisions on an individual project basis without consideration of the cumulative effect of many such decisions. For example, the removal of a few hectares of rainforest or a small portion of coral reef as part of one development project may not be highly significant in and of itself, but the cumulative effect of many such projects may have important repercussions.

Often, an overall country or regional plan is needed which can be consulted to ensure that such issues are dealt with appropriately.

Cultural, Historical and Aesthetic Resources

Many development projects not only entail the modification of natural habitats but may also have adverse effects on culturally or historically significant sites. Other projects will result in the loss of scenic resources. In many instances, these aspects of a project may have important implications in terms of its acceptance by local residents.

Losses of cultural or historical resources are difficult to quantify and monetize because the perception of these losses depend on cultural traditions and value systems. The contingent valuation techniques described in Chapter 6 are one way of estimating the values of these resources, but the limitations inherent in these techniques make it difficult to arrive at meaningful estimates. For example, attempts to determine local residents' willingness to accept compensation for the loss of an important cultural site may show that they are unwilling to accept any level of compensation, no matter how high. Though their willingness to pay to keep the site may be constrained by income, the amount needed to compensate them for such a loss may be extremely high, or even infinite.

Aesthetic resources represent similar measurement problems, though the values involved are likely to be much smaller. In these cases, either the property-value approach or the contingent valuation methods can be applied to obtain estimates.

When such issues threaten to have significant impacts on project acceptance, compromises may be necessary. These may involve moving the site of the project, moving the cultural or historical relic to a nearby site, or some other form of mitigation measure to reduce the losses involved. The relocation of Abu Simbel and other historic treasures in Egypt when they were threatened by the rising waters of the Aswan High Dam is one notable example.

Summary

Despite the limitations to economic analysis of the environmental impacts of development projects, it is important that such impacts be included in the analyses. In many cases the techniques described in the preceding chapters can be extremely useful in providing more accurate estimates of the value of the impacts of development on the environment and, therefore, in generating more accurate and balanced appraisals of the proposed projects. Where environmental assessment with economic valuation fails completely to capture certain impacts on the environment, these impacts may at least be included qualitatively in the project analysis.

The candid discussion in this chapter of some problem areas in the evaluation of environmental impacts should not be taken to mean that the techniques for valuation are ineffectual. Many developmental impacts on the environment may be valued and included in economic analyses by using the techniques described in this book. The challenge is twofold – the identification of major impacts on the environment from development projects, and the valuation and incorporation of these impacts into project analysis.

Appendix: Case Studies

The five case studies in this appendix illustrate some of the valuation techniques introduced in the text. Not all the data needed for the analyses were available, although some of them should have been easy to obtain at the time of the original appraisals had the need been recognized. Where actual data were not available, synthetic but realistic data have been substituted.

The first case uses changes in the values of milk, fertilizer and firewood production to assess a watershed management and forest development project in Nepal. The second compares the cost-effectiveness of several waste-water disposal methods for a proposed geothermal plant in the Philippines. A Thai fishery project and unintended depletion of resources as a consequence is described in the third case. The fourth is a note on the environmental effects of the disposal of effluent from an Indonesian palm oil mill. The last case study examines on-site and off-site effects of alternative land-management approaches in the uplands of Northern Thailand. It should be noted that most of the economic measurement of environmental effects presented here rely on physical changes in the production of goods and services which are valued by using market prices; they are examples of those techniques labeled "generally applicable" in Chapter 4.

Case Study 1: Nepal Hill Forest Development Project

This case study, based on an Asian Development Bank project appraisal report and on reports of a similar project by Fleming (1983) (also found in Hufschmidt *et al.*, 1983), is a description of the benefit valuation for a benefit-cost analysis of a management program for two watersheds in Nepal. It is an example of the use of change-in-productivity techniques in which actual market prices are used as a measure for valuing the benefits of environmental improvements. In this example, physical changes in production brought about by the project are valued using market or, where appropriate, shadow prices for inputs and for outputs. The productivity effects of both introducing the project and of not doing so (with- and without-project analysis) are evaluated. Both on-site and off-site effects are included in the analysis.

INTRODUCTION TO THE PROJECT

The forests of Nepal are continually being degraded by overcutting and overgrazing; the results are inadequate and polluted water supplies, shortages of fuelwood and leaf fodder, and increasing soil erosion.

The major causes of the overexploitation of the forests around Kathmandu and Pokhara are the need of the rural population for greater income and the shortage of fuelwood in the urban settlements. Most of the forests in the middle hills, where 52 percent of the population live, have been converted into shrubland. Trees are being cut down or lopped heavily and the forest floor is overgrazed. The shrubland is being exploited for fodder and stripped of fuelwood. As a result, the water-retaining capacity of natural vegetation in the hill forests has been reduced and runoff has increased in both quantity and speed. Each year an estimated 240 million cubic meters (m^3) of eroded soil is transported downstream by the country's major rivers and their tributaries, causing major damage.

The introduction of systematic hill-forest management was proposed to help meet the fuelwood and fodder requirements of rural and urban communities and to reduce the effects of downstream siltation. The project area is 38,500 hectares, of which 10,000 hectares are used for agriculture and 1,500 for pasture. The management component of the project is concerned only with the remaining 27,000 hectares of forested and grazing land: 22,000 of these hectares are made up of three forest ranges in the Kathmandu Forest Division (KFD) and the other 5,000 are two forest beats in the Pokhara Forest Division (PFD). These two forest divisions are major catchment areas of the Bagmati and Seti rivers and serve the urban centers of Kathmandu and Pokhara.

Among the elements of the project are:
  (i) Management planning for the entire area which includes forest inventory, preparation of working plans and the delineation of land-use compartments in the forest;
 (ii) Shrubland and timber-stand improvement which includes the tending of 16,000 hectares of shrubland, the improvement of 7,000 hectares of timber stand and additional fencing within the total 27,000 hectares of forest; and
(iii) Afforestation of 4,000 hectares of grasslands within the total forest area with species for both fuelwood and fodder as well as for fencing materials.

Subsistence agriculture is the main economic activity in the area. The principal crops are rice, maize, millet, wheat, potatoes and other vegetables. The average holding is half a hectare. Buffalo and cattle are kept for milk, manure and ploughing. Feed for livestock is made up of agricultural residues (about 50 percent) and fodder from the forests. The forests also provide fuelwood and timber.

LAND USE WITHOUT THE PROJECT: PROJECTIONS

Population growth, accentuated by urbanization, is reducing state forests around Kathmandu and Pokhara. The three main demands that this produces on the forest are for fuelwood – both for home and industrial use – fodder and grazing for livestock, and land for agriculture. With the average consumption of fuelwood at around one cubic meter *per capita* per year, the total demand is estimated at around 8–9 million cubic meters per year. An estimate of fuelwood production in the forests around Kathmandu and Pokhara puts the annual sustained production at well below the amount required. The deficit is met by importing wood from the Terai, the illegal removal of wood from the surrounding forests, or by using cattle dung as a substitute. The illegal removal and sale of firewood and leaf fodder from government forests is a major source of income for the local population of the area of the proposed project and is the main reason why the forests are being denuded. The use of cattle dung as fuel diminishes the already scarce supply of fertilizer for agricultural production.

Given that the population is growing at the rate of 2.6 percent per annum and that there is no foreseeable increase in agricultural productivity, the pressure to convert forest to agricultural land will continue. There is also a considerable pressure to convert forests into grazing land to support the growing numbers of livestock.

Table A.1: Projected Land Use with and without Project, Five-Year Intervals 1983–2022 (in hectares; after Fleming, 1983)

Land Use without Project	1983	1988	1993	1998	2022
Agriculture	10,000	13,730	15,769	18,424	26,848
Grazing	4,000	4,520	5,107	5,771	7,475
Pasture	1,500	1,500	1,500	1,500	1,500
Scrubland	16,000	13,830	13,555	12,805	2,677
Forest	7,000	4,920	2,569	0	0
Land Use with Project[a]	1983	1988	1993	1998	2022
Agriculture	10,000	10,000	10,000	10,000	10,000
Grazing	4,000	0	0	0	0
Pasture	1,500	1,500	1,500	1,500	1,500
Scrubland[b]	16,000	16,000	16,000	16,000	16,000
Forest[b]	7,000	7,000	7,000	7,000	7,000
Plantations[b]	0	4,000	4,000	4,000	4,000

[a] Assumes existence of a separate agricultural management plan that eliminates the need to convert land to agriculture.
[b] See Table A.5 for project production projections.
Note: Actual data were not available; data shown are synthetic.

Projections show that the present rates of use, together with increased pressure from a growing population, will, within fourteen years, destroy the entire forested area of the Nepalese hills, some 2.5 million hectares. Without the project, therefore, as a consequence of the indiscriminate removal of the vegetation, the water-retaining capacity of the area would continue to decline, water runoff would increase both in velocity and volume, and even greater siltation problems would emerge below the hills.

Land-use projections, both with and without the project, are given in Table A.1.

PROJECTED LAND USE WITH THE PROJECT

It is assumed that a separate agricultural program would increase productivity on existing cultivated lands at rates equal to, or greater than, the rate of population increase and that the amount of agricultural land would remain constant at 10,000 hectares. No grazing, pasture, scrubland or forest would be converted into terraces.

The project will contribute significantly to the control of erosion, landslides and flash floods. Establishing vegetative cover on barren hill slopes will improve the water regime by increasing the recharge of aquifers. However, these types of benefit are not easily quantifiable.

The project will also help to alleviate shortages in fuelwood and livestock fodder in the Kathmandu and Pokhara valleys. Further, it will reduce the incidence of the destructive and illegal removal of forest products by soliciting community co-operation in forest protection. It will also help to improve overall agricultural productivity in the area once livestock dung, currently used as fuel because of wood shortages, is applied as fertilizer.

VALUATION OF BENEFITS

The project is planned to reduce soil erosion, to increase the productivity of the different land uses within the watershed and to provide a sustainable flow of resources which would include fuelwood and fodder. Benefit-cost analysis, based on estimates of the economic values of the products from differing uses of land, can be used to assess the project. The benefits of the program may be considered to be equal to the land values (the economic value of the products) achieved with the project, minus the land values without the project. These benefits and costs can then be used to calculate the EIRR in the usual manner. The main problem is in valuing the differing outputs from the various uses of land, a problem considered in the following pages. The calculations are based on the values in Tables A.2 and A.3.

DETERMINATION OF LAND-USE VALUES

Grazing Land. Grazing animals produce milk and fertilizer. Given the values in Tables A.2 and A.3 and assuming a fodder consumption rate of 14,000 kilograms per

Table A.2: Per Hectare Production of Various Products (Without Project)

	Grazing Land	Pasture Land	Unmanaged Scrubland	Unmanaged Forest
Grass (kg/ha/yr)	1,200	6,000	500	—
Tree foliage (kg/ha/yr)	—	—	700	1,400
Wood (m³/ha/yr)	—	—	1	2.2

Table A.3: Production and Value of Animal Products

	Fertilizer Production per Animal per year (kg)	1983 Value (Rs/kg)		Milk Production per 1,000 kg feed (l)	1983 Value (Rs/l)
Nitrogen (N)	15	6	Grass feed	60	1.5
Phosphorous (P)	2	18	Foliage feed	120	1.5

l = liter

animal per year, the annual value of fertilizer production is calculated to be 126 rupees per animal per year or 11 rupees per hectare per year, Rs/ha/yr. This figure is found by determining the value of the fertilizer produced per animal from Table A.3 and multiplying this amount by the carrying capacity of one hectare of land. In the case of grazing land, the carrying capacity is .0857 based on grass production on grazing land, 1,200kg, divided by the annual feed requirement per animal, 14,000kg. Similarly, the annual value of milk production per hectare of grazing land can be calculated to be 108 Rs/ha/yr. The total annual productive value of grazing land would, therefore, be the total of the values of milk and fertilizer production or 119 Rs/ha/yr.

Since market prices are used to establish fertilizer and milk values per hectare of grazing land, it is important to confirm that these prices reflect the true opportunity cost or marginal willingness to pay. Any input-price subsidies should be added to the price and if milk prices are controlled by the government, alternative prices which more accurately reflect marginal willingness to pay should be obtained.

Pasture. Since fodder production from pasture is estimated to be five times that of grazing land, the annual value from pasture would be 595 Rs/ha/yr.

Unmanaged Scrubland. The production data for scrubland (degraded forest land) are given in Table A.2. From these data it was calculated that the annual value of fertilizer produced from scrubland grass was 5 Rs/ha/yr and that the annual value of the milk was 45 Rs/ha/yr.

Assuming that the average grazing animal consumes about 7,100 kilograms of tree foliage per year, the value of the fertilizer so produced on scrubland was calculated at 12 Rs/ha/yr and the milk production at 126 Rs/ha/yr. Taking production from both grass and tree foliage together, each hectare of unmanaged scrubland could, therefore, produce Rs17 worth of fertilizer and Rs171 worth of milk each year.

Fuelwood is produced on both scrub and forest lands. Three methods were presented in order to estimate fuelwood values.

Direct Market-Value Approach. In 1983 the economic price for fuelwood (the market price minus the cost of bringing wood to the market) in Pokhara and Kathmandu, the principal marketplaces, was 560 Rs per metric ton (mt). Assuming an average wood density of 500 kg/m^3, fuelwood would be worth 280 Rs/m^3, (500 kg/m^3 × 0.001 mt/kg × 560 Rs/mt). At present, the Fuelwood Corporation of Nepal (FCN) is supplying only 2 percent and 8 percent, respectively, of the total fuelwood for all of Nepal and Kathmandu valleys. Unless the FCN finds an alternative source of supply, market prices for fuelwood are expected to rise. The project's production would represent approximately 20 percent of the current fuelwood consumption in Kathmandu. Because the fuelwood markets are small and isolated, the market price may not represent the value of fuelwood outside the market. Therefore two other indirect measures of fuelwood value were made.

Indirect Substitute Approach. Fuelwood can also be valued in terms of the value of alternative uses of its closest substitute (for example, cattle dung which can be dried and burned when wood is unavailable). The opportunity cost of using cattle dung as fuel rather than fertilizer can be estimated in terms of the losses in foodgrain production. This would be based on the following assumptions:
  (i) 1 m^3 of wood is the energy equivalent of 0.6 ton of dried cattle dung or 2.4 tons of fresh manure;
  (ii) an average family uses 6 tons per year of fresh manure on 0.5 ha of cultivated land;
  (iii) the increase in maize yields expected as a result of using dung as fertilizer would be 15 percent, which gives an opportunity cost of Rs27 per ton of fresh manure, assuming that the increase in maize yields is from 1.53 mt/ha to 1.8 mt/ha and that the price of maize equals 1,200 Rs/mt. The value of fuelwood would thus be Rs65 per m^3.

Indirect Opportunity-Cost Approach. The third method is an opportunity-cost approach based on the time families spend carrying fuelwood from the forest, and assumes that fuelwood is a common property resource. This method is based on the following assumptions:
  (i) 30kg of fuelwood are collected daily by each family;

(ii) each family spends an average of 132 workdays per year collecting fuel-wood. Assuming an average wood density of 500 kg/m³, each family gathers 7.92 m³ of fuelwood per year (132 person days × 0.06 m³ per day). At a daily gathering wage of Rs5 (the opportunity cost of labor based on other employment), the estimated value is calculated to be 83 Rs/m³. The value of fuelwood as estimated in the three approaches is therefore as follows:

Method	Value (Rs/m³)
Direct-Market Value	280
Indirect-Substitute	65
Indirect-Opportunity Cost	83

The most conservative estimate (the lowest) was chosen for the analysis. Therefore, the annual fuelwood value per hectare of unmanaged scrubland would be 65 Rs/ha/yr (based on production of 1 m³/ha/yr, Table A.2). The *total* annual value of scrubland was estimated to be the value of the milk, fertilizer and fuelwood, or a total of 253 Rs/ha/yr.

Unmanaged Forest. This land is open to restricted grazing and harvesting of fuelwood and fodder. The annual value of the fertilizer was estimated to be 25 Rs/ha/yr and the annual value of milk 252 Rs/ha/yr. Using the indirect-substitute method, the annual value of fuelwood was estimated to be 143 Rs/ha/yr. The total annual value of unmanaged forest would therefore be 420 Rs/ha/yr. The per hectare values for grazing, pasture, unmanaged scrub and unmanaged forest land are summarized in Table A.4.

Table A.4: Per Hectare Values of Various Products without the Project (Rs/ha/yr)

Land Use	Milk	Fertilizer	Fuelwood	Total
Grazing	108	11	—	119
Pasture	540	55	—	595
Unmanaged Scrub	171	17	65	253
Unmanaged Forest	252	25	143	420

LAND VALUES WITH THE PROJECT

Based on calculations similar to those used when considering land use without the project, the per hectare physical yields on land affected by the project are given in Table A.5. Physical yields were translated into economic values based on the values of the fuelwood, fertilizer and milk produced. These results are summarized in Table A.6.

Table A.5: Projected Yields with Project (tons/ha)

Operational Year	Plantations	Managed Scrubland	Managed Forest
Fuelwood			
1	0	1.2	5.5
2	0	0	0
3	0	2.5	0
4	0	0	0
5	0	2.0	0
6	20.0	0	22.5
7–9	0	0	0
10	0	5.2	0
11	8.0	0	25.0
12–15	8.0	0	0
16	8.0	0	27.5
17–19	8.0	0	0
20	8.0	20.0	0
21	8.0	0	27.5
22–25	8.0	0	0
26	8.0	0	27.5
27–29	8.0	0	0
30	8.0	35.0	0
31	8.0	0	27.5
32–34	8.0	0	0
35	8.0	35.0	0
36–40	8.0	0	36.2
Fodder			
1–5	2.0	0.7	1.4
6–10	5.6	0.9	1.6
11–15	5.6	1.3	3.0
16–20	5.6	1.7	3.3
21–25	5.6	2.1	3.3
26–40	5.6	2.7	3.3

Note: (tons/ha $\times$ 2 = m^3/ha; tons/ha $\times$ 1000 = kg/ha).
Source: Asian Development Bank, *Appraisal of the Hill Forest Development Project in the Kingdom of Nepal* (1983).

ANALYSIS

The total land values under each management alternative can be calculated by multiplying the number of hectares of each type of land by their values. The types of land are shown in Table A.1, the values without the project are given in Table A.4 and those with the project in Table A.6. The per hectare values of grazing and

Table A.6: Per Hectare Values of Various Products with Project (Rs/ha/yr)

Operational Year	Plantations	Managed Scrubland	Managed Forest
Fuelwood			
1	0	156	715
2	0	0	0
3	0	325	0
4	0	0	0
5	0	260	0
6	2,600	0	2,925
7–9	0	0	0
10	0	676	0
11	1,040	0	3,250
12–15	1,040	0	0
16	1,040	0	3,575
17–19	1,040	0	0
20	1,040	2,600	0
21	1,040	0	3,575
22–25	1,040	0	0
26	1,040	0	3,575
27–29	1,040	0	0
30	1,040	4,550	0
31	1,040	0	3,575
32–34	1,040	0	0
35	1,040	4,550	0
36	1,040	0	4,706
37–40	1,040	0	0
Milk			
1–5	360	126	252
6–10	1,008	162	288
11–15	1,008	234	540
16–20	1,008	306	594
21–25	1,008	378	594
26–40	1,008	486	594
Fertilizer			
1–5	35	12	25
6–10	99	16	28
11–15	99	23	53
16–20	99	30	59
21–25	99	37	59
26–40	99	48	59

Table A.7:   Total Value for Unmanaged Lands (Rs)

	Grazing			Scrubland			Forest			Total Value
Yr	ha	Rs/ha	Rs	ha	Rs/ha	Rs	ha	Rs/ha	Rs	
1	4,000	119	476,000	16,000	253	4,048,000	7,000	420	2,940,000	7,464,000
2	4,104	119	488,376	15,566	253	3,938,198	6,584	420	2,765,280	7,191,854
3	4,208	119	500,752	15,132	253	3,828,396	6,168	420	2,590,560	6,919,708
4	4,312	119	513,128	14,698	253	3,718,594	5,752	420	2,415,840	6,647,562
5	4,416	119	525,504	14,264	253	3,608,792	5,336	420	2,241,120	6,375,416
6	4,520	119	537,880	13,830	253	3,498,990	4,920	420	2,066,400	6,103,270
7	4,638	119	551,922	13,775	253	3,485,075	4,450	420	1,869,000	5,905,997
8	4,755	119	565,845	13,720	253	3,471,160	3,980	420	1,671,600	5,708,605
9	4,872	119	579,768	13,665	253	3,457,245	3,510	420	1,474,200	5,511,213
10	4,990	119	593,810	13,610	253	3,443,330	3,040	420	1,276,800	5,313,940
11	5,107	119	607,733	13,555	253	3,429,415	2,569	420	1,078,980	5,116,128
12	5,240	119	623,560	13,405	253	3,391,465	2,056	420	863,520	4,878,545
13	5,373	119	639,387	13,255	253	3,353,515	1,542	420	647,640	4,640,542
14	5,506	119	655,214	13,105	253	3,315,565	1,028	420	431,760	4,402,539
15	5,639	119	671,041	12,955	253	3,277,615	514	420	215,880	4,164,536
16	5,771	119	686,749	12,805	253	3,239,665	0	420	0	3,926,414
17	5,842	119	695,198	12,383	253	3,132,899				3,828,097
18	5,913	119	703,647	11,961	253	3,026,133				3,729,780
19	5,984	119	712,096	11,539	253	2,919,367				3,631,463
20	6,055	119	720,545	11,117	253	2,812,601				3,533,146
21	6,126	119	728,994	10,695	253	2,705,835				3,434,829
22	6,197	119	737,443	10,273	253	2,599,069				3,336,512
23	6,268	119	745,892	9,851	253	2,492,303				3,238,195
24	6,339	119	754,341	9,429	253	2,385,537				3,139,878
25	6,410	119	762,790	9,007	253	2,278,771				3,041,561
26	6,481	119	771,239	8,585	253	2,172,005				2,943,244
27	6,552	119	779,688	8,163	206	2,065,239				2,844,927
28	6,623	119	788,137	7,741	253	1,958,473				2,746,610
29	6,694	119	796,586	7,319	253	1,851,707				2,648,293
30	6,765	119	805,035	6,897	253	1,744,941				2,549,976
31	6,836	119	813,484	6,475	253	1,638,175				2,451,659
32	6,907	119	821,933	6,053	253	1,531,409				2,353,342
33	6,978	119	830,382	5,631	253	1,424,643				2,255,025
34	7,049	119	838,831	5,209	253	1,317,877				2,156,708
35	7,120	119	847,280	4,787	253	1,211,111				2,058,391
36	7,191	119	855,729	4,365	253	1,104,345				1,960,074
37	7,262	119	864,178	3,943	253	997,579				1,861,757
38	7,333	119	872,627	3,521	253	890,813				1,763,440
39	7,404	119	881,076	3,099	253	784,047				1,665,213
40	7,475	119	889,525	2,677	253	677,281				1,566,806

Table A.8: Total Value for Managed Lands (Rs)

Yr	Plantations			Scrubland			Forest			Grazing			Total Value
	Rs/ha	ha	Rs	Rs/ha	ha	Rs	Rs/ha	ha	Rs	Rs/ha	ha	Rs	
1	395	1,000	395,000	294	16,000	4,704,000	992	7,000	69,444,000	119	4,000	476,000	12,519,000
2	395	2,000	790,000	138	16,000	2,208,000	277	7,000	1,939,000	119	3,000	357,000	5,294,000
3	395	3,000	1,185,000	463	16,000	7,408,000	277	7,000	1,939,000	119	2,000	238,000	10,770,000
4	395	4,000	1,580,000	138	16,000	2,208,000	277	7,000	1,939,000	119	1,000	119,000	5,846,000
5	395	4,000	1,580,000	398	16,000	6,368,000	277	7,000	1,939,000	119			9,887,000
6	3,707	4,000	14,828,000	178	16,000	2,848,000	3,241	7,000	22,687,000				40,363,000
7	1,107	4,000	4,428,000	178	16,000	2,848,000	316	7,000	2,212,000				9,488,000
8	1,107	4,000	4,428,000	178	16,000	2,848,000	316	7,000	2,212,000				9,488,000
9	1,107	4,000	4,428,000	178	16,000	2,848,000	316	7,000	2,212,000				9,488,000
10	1,107	4,000	4,428,000	854	16,000	13,664,000	316	7,000	2,212,000				20,304,000
11	2,147	4,000	8,588,000	257	16,000	4,112,000	3,843	7,000	26,901,000				39,601,000
12	2,147	4,000	8,588,000	257	16,000	4,112,000	593	7,000	4,151,000				16,851,000
13	2,147	4,000	8,588,000	257	16,000	4,112,000	593	7,000	4,151,000				16,851,000
14	2,147	4,000	8,588,000	257	16,000	4,112,000	593	7,000	4,151,000				16,851,000
15	2,147	4,000	8,588,000	257	16,000	5,376,000	593	7,000	4,151,000				16,851,000
16	2,147	4,000	8,588,000	336	16,000	5,376,000	4,228	7,000	29,596,000				4,356,000
17	2,147	4,000	8,588,000	336	16,000	5,376,000	653	7,000	4,571,000				1,853,500
18	2,147	4,000	8,588,000	336	16,000	5,376,000	653	7,000	4,571,000				1,853,500
19	2,147	4,000	8,588,000	336	16,000	5,376,000	653	7,000	4,571,000				1,853,500
20	2,147	4,000	8,588,000	2,936	16,000	46,976,000	653	7,000	4,571,000				60,135,000
21	2,147	4,000	8,588,000	415	16,000	6,640,000	4,228	7,000	29,596,000				44,824,000
22	2,147	4,000	8,588,000	415	16,000	6,640,000	653	7,000	4,571,000				19,799,000
23	2,147	4,000	8,588,000	415	16,000	6,640,000	653	7,000	4,571,000				19,799,000
24	2,147	4,000	8,588,000	415	16,000	6,640,000	653	7,000	4,571,000				19,799,000
25	2,147	4,000	8,588,000	415	16,000	6,640,000	653	7,000	4,571,000				19,799,000
26	2,147	4,000	8,588,000	534	16,000	8,544,000	4,228	7,000	29,596,000				46,728,000
27	2,147	4,000	8,588,000	534	16,000	8,544,000	653	7,000	4,571,000				21,703,000
28	2,147	4,000	8,588,000	534	16,000	8,544,000	653	7,000	4,571,000				21,703,000
29	2,147	4,000	8,588,000	534	16,000	8,544,000	653	7,000	4,571,000				21,703,000
30	2,147	4,000	8,588,000	5,084	16,000	81,344,000	653	7,000	4,571,000				94,503,000
31	2,147	4,000	8,588,000	534	16,000	8,544,000	4,228	7,000	29,596,000				46,728,000
32	2,147	4,000	8,588,000	534	16,000	8,544,000	653	7,000	4,571,000				21,703,000
33	2,147	4,000	8,588,000	534	16,000	8,544,000	653	7,000	4,571,000				21,703,000
34	2,147	4,000	8,588,000	534	16,000	8,544,000	653	7,000	4,571,000				21,703,000
35	2,147	4,000	8,588,000	5,084	16,000	81,344,000	653	7,000	4,571,000				94,503,000
36	2,147	4,000	8,588,000	534	16,000	8,544,000	4,228	7,000	29,596,000				46,728,000
37	2,147	4,000	8,588,000	534	16,000	8,544,000	653	7,000	4,571,000				21,703,000
38	2,147	4,000	8,588,000	534	16,000	8,544,000	653	7,000	4,571,000				21,703,000
39	2,147	4,000	8,588,000	534	16,000	8,544,000	653	7,000	4,571,000				21,703,000
40	2,147	4,000	8,588,000	534	16,000	8,544,000	653	7,000	4,571,000				21,703,000

Table A.9: Economic Evaluation: Benefit-Cost Streams (Rs'000)

Year	Cost [a]	Incremental Benefits	Net Benefits
1	22,597	5,055	−17,542
2	27,128	−1,898	−29,026
3	28,648	3,850	−24,798
4	27,616	−802	−28,448
5	32,246	3,512	−28,734
6	34,604	34,260	−344
7	8,996	3,582	−5,414
8	9,183	3,779	−5,404
9	5,278	3,977	−1,301
10	5,763	14,990	9,227
11	3,309	34,485	31,176
12	3,215	12,448	8,757
13	3,120	12,210	9,090
14	3,215	12,448	9,233
15	3,309	12,686	9,377
16	3,403	14,805	36,231
17	3,498	14,707	11,209
18	3,402	14,805	11,402
19	3,309	14,904	11,595
20	3,215	56,602	53,387
21	3,120	41,389	38,269
22	3,215	16,462	13,247
23	3,309	16,561	13,252
24	3,403	16,659	13,256
25	3,498	16,757	13,259
26	3,403	43,785	40,382
27	3,309	18,858	15,549
28	3,215	18,956	15,741
29	3,120	19,055	15,935
30	3,215	91,953	88,738
31	3,309	44,276	40,967
32	3,403	19,350	15,947
33	3,498	19,448	15,950
34	3,403	19,546	16,143
35	3,309	92,445	89,136
36	3,215	44,768	41,553
37	3,120	19,841	16,721
38	3,215	19,940	16,725
39	3,309	20,038	16,729
40	3,403	20,136	16,733

[a] Project costs are given in ADB, *Appraisal of the Hill Forest Development Project (1983)* and represent the initial project costs and continuing management expenses for the project.
Note: Economic internal rate of return (EIRR) = 8.5 percent.

pasture land are assumed to be the same in both cases. Total land values for unmanaged lands (without the project) are given in Table A.7. Table A.8 gives the with-project, managed-lands figures.

The contribution of the project to the control of soil erosion, landslides and flooding is not accurately quantifiable and is therefore not included in this analysis. The incremental benefits of the management program are assumed to be the difference between the values of products from the unmanaged land (that is, without the proposed scheme) and the values of products if the management scheme is adopted. In each case the value of agricultural production is assumed to be constant. The incremental benefits of the project, minus its costs, result in a stream of net benefits which yield an EIRR of 8.5 percent (see Table A.9).

This case illustrates the use of valuation techniques to place monetary values on a change in pasture and scrubland/forest productivity brought about by a project. A with-and-without-project framework was used to determine the scale of productivity changes. Both direct and indirect methods were used to estimate prices for the fertilizer, milk and fuelwood produced.

Case Study 2: Tongonan Geothermal Power Plant, Leyte, Philippines

The complete case study, of which this is a part, was adapted by Somluckrat Grandstaff from materials prepared by Beta Balagot, and may be found in Dixon and Hufschmidt (1986). It presents the analysis of the cost-effectiveness of various options for disposing of waste water from a geothermal power plant built on the island of Leyte in the Philippines. The decision to build the power plant and to tap the local geothermal energy had already been made; it was necessary to decide which means of waste-water disposal from the plant would protect the environment in the most cost-effective manner. The cost-effectiveness approach is discussed in Chapter 4.

Seven ways of disposing of waste water are considered in the full case study; the costs of building and operating each are different and each has a different effect on the environment. The analysis examines each option in turn, determining its monetary values and, where possible, its environmental effect.

Not all of the effects on the environment can be quantified and monetized, but those which cannot be quantified should not be ignored in the analysis. These effects are listed in a qualitative manner and taken into consideration when the final decision is made. In this way the decision-maker or project designer is presented with a range of information on the actual costs of construction and operation of each option as well as the various effects of each upon the environment.

While each option is subjected to a complete benefit-cost analysis, a more complete presentation would include a benefit-cost analysis of the entire project including the differing options for design of the power plant as a whole as well as those for disposing of waste water. In this way the economic worth of the entire

FIGURE A.1: *Location of Tongonan Geothermal Field, Leyte*

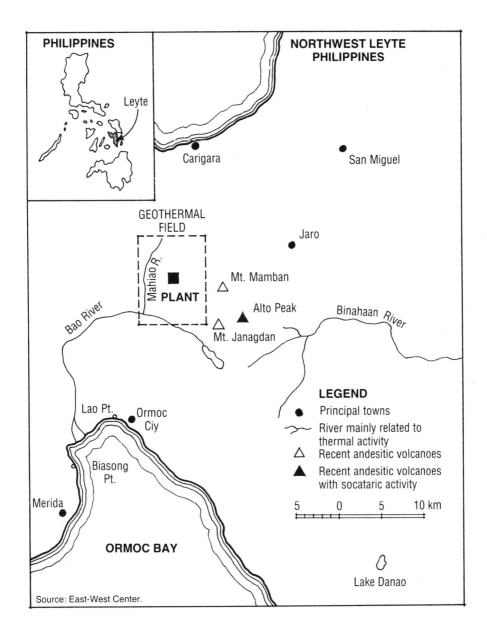

project, not just one part of it, could have been explored and then compared with other ways of producing electricity.

BACKGROUND INFORMATION

In the past the Philippines has been highly dependent on imported crude oil to meet its energy requirements and so has adopted an energy policy which will promote various forms of domestic energy production. These include nuclear energy, hydro-electric power, coal, petroleum, natural gas and geothermal energy. This last is derived from the natural heat of the earth. With existing technology only geothermal reservoirs associated with recent hot intrusive rocks and with vulcanism can be harnessed for the generation of electrical power. High-temperature geothermal energy is found in two forms: dry-steam fields, as seen in the geysers of the United States, and hot-water (wet) fields, as seen at Wairakei and Broadland in New Zealand. At present the Philippines is exploiting only the wet fields which produce a mix of steam and water.

Exploration at Tongonan in Leyte started in 1973, and in 1978 a potential productive capacity of 3,000 MW of geothermal electricity was confirmed. This case study considers Phase I of the Tongonan Geothermal Power Plant (TGPP) which has a capacity of 112.5 MW (see Figure A.1). This power station relies on a wet-steam geothermal resource and produces residual liquids and gases. These have chemical and thermal characteristics that may affect the environment adversely; the degree to which they might do so depends on the rate and frequency of discharge and the method of disposal.

ENVIRONMENTAL DIMENSIONS

An Environmental Impact Report prepared by Kingston, Reynolds, Thom and Allardice Limited (KRTA), consultants to the Ministry of Energy and the Philippine National Oil Corporation, indicated that the major adverse effects on the environment would be caused by the disposal of the geothermal waste fluids. The fluids from the Tongonan wells contain more dissolved solids than those from most other geothermal fields; these include chloride, silica, arsenic, boron and lithium. Arsenic, boron, lithium and mercury all have known toxic effects on plants, animals and people, and the full case study examines these effects. The indiscriminate disposal of geothermal waste water would have severe effects on health and productivity and, to minimize these, the government has set limits to its discharge. Concentrations of arsenic, boron and lithium in water from the Tongonan wells were found to exceed the limits recommended by the National Pollution Control Commission.

Although the full case study examined the costs and benefits of all seven methods of disposing of the waste water, our abbreviated version will outline the analysis of only four of them; the analysis of the remainder may be found in Dixon and Hufschmidt (1986).

THE DATA

Seven options for disposal for the waste water of the plant were proposed:

(1) Reinjection.

(2) Discharge into the Mahiao River without treatment.

(3) Discharge into the Mahiao River after treatment for the removal of arsenic.

(4) Discharge into the Bao River without treatment.

(5) Discharge into the Bao River after treatment for the removal of arsenic.

(6) Discharge at sea without treatment through an outfall at Lao Point.

(7) Discharge at sea without treatment through an outfall at Biasong Point.

In the first option, geothermal fluids from separator stations would be piped to reinjection wells within the field. At full capacity the 112.5 MW power plant would need seven such wells. A standby disposal system consisting of thermal ponds and other contingency structures would also be needed. They would be used while the reinjection system was temporarily shut down either for maintenance or for some limited emergency. When the system is shut down for longer periods the stand-by scheme would permit the discharge of chemically treated waste fluids into the river.

The second and third options involve the direct discharge of waste fluids into the Mahiao River (see Figure A.1). Before being discharged the fluids would be retained for a few days in a thermal pond where they may be treated with chemicals to remove arsenic.

In Options (4) and (5) waste fluids would be discharged into the Bao River through a pipeline. A thermal pond would also be required for cooling the fluids before releasing them into the river. Option (5) would entail treatment of the fluids in the pond in order to precipitate the arsenic.

Options (6) and (7) involve the selection of an outfall at sea through which to discharge the wastes. Two possible sites have been studied: Lao Point and the Biasong Point. An outfall at the former would involve 22 kilometers of pipeline and at the latter 32 kilometers.

COSTS AND ENVIRONMENTAL EFFECTS OF THE OPTIONS

Each of the seven options has different capital and operations, maintenance and replacement (OM&R) costs as well as different effects on the environment. These are briefly described here and 1980 prices are used in the analysis.

(1) Reinjection. The construction of seven reinjection wells and the stand-by waste-disposal system will take two years. Each well will cost P10 million, or P70 million in all. The construction of a system of pipelines from the separator stations to the reinjection wells will cost P20 million. The stand-by waste-disposal system will involve another P17 million. The annual operation and maintenance costs will total P10.4 million.

Although reinjection is seen as the most ecologically sound method of disposal, it

101

is not yet a well-established technology. In areas where water supplies are drawn from underground aquifers, as in the site of this project, it is important to know the local groundwater hydrology and to monitor carefully any effects of injecting geothermal waste water.

Reinjection may also lower the temperature and hence the potential energy of the sub-surface geothermal water. In addition the geothermal liquids at Tongonan contain large amounts of dissolved solids like silica which may clog the reinjection pipes. Such problems could be dealt with by adding chemicals to keep the solids in solution, but the effect of these chemicals may be to create other environmental problems.

(2) Discharge into the Mahiao River without treatment. The construction of a thermal pond would take one year and cost P7 million. Operation and maintenance costs are estimated at P43,300 per year (P0.0433 million).

High levels of arsenic and boron in the untreated waste fluids discharged into the river would affect adversely the productivity of 4,000 hectares of rice fields served by the Bao River Irrigation System.

If the irrigation waters are heavily polluted, farmers will probably not irrigate their crops; the consequence is a severe reduction in productivity. Irrigated rice fields yield an average of 61 cavans (1 cavan = 50kg) per hectare against a yield of 37.9 cavans from unirrigated fields (NIA Region 8 Office, 1980). Production would also be reduced to one crop a year. However, since the rice produced in the Bao River Irrigation System is only a small part of the regional total, it can safely be assumed that these changes in production will not affect local rice prices.

Based on the cost of production data for the area over the 1975–78 period, the net return per hectare for irrigated rice was estimated at P346 and for unirrigated rice, P324. If irrigation water were made unusable for the entire 4,000 hectares, the economic loss would be as follows:

$$4,000 \text{ ha} \times \text{P346 per ha} \times 2 \text{ crops} = \text{P2,768,000}$$

One crop of unirrigated rice could be grown, yielding the following net return:

$$4,000 \text{ ha} \times \text{P324} = \text{P1,296,000}$$

The annual loss, therefore, would be the difference, P1.47 million.

An added environmental cost of discharging untreated waste water into the river system is the risk to human health and livestock. To evaluate this, the cost of a water-purification system that will render the river water safe for domestic use and for drinking was also estimated. The construction of such a system would cost P50 million and cost P15 million annually to operate and maintain.

Estimating the costs to the freshwater ecosystem is more difficult, since there are no data on the economic value of the fishing along the river. However, another

102

environmental cost which can be estimated will be the pollution of the delta, which will affect the marine fisheries of the area. The delta or mangrove area of Ormoc Bay plays an important role in sustaining productivity in the adjoining fishing grounds because it is the feeding and spawning ground of several species of fish.

Fishing is an important industry in the Ormoc Bay–Camotes Sea area. Based on 1978 figures, the net return from fishing was estimated at 29 percent of the gross return from the catch. Although the annual value of the fish catch varied from year to year depending on the actual size of the catch and on market prices, a gross value of P39.4 million was taken as representative. If this fishery was lost as a consequence of heavy-metal contamination, the annual economic loss would be about P11.4 million (P39.4 × 0.29). It is assumed that the capital equipment could be sold or shifted to other areas, but that the lost catch would not be replaced by additional fish catches elsewhere.

(3) Discharge to Mahiao River After Treatment. A thermal pond will be constructed at a cost of P7 million and completed in one year. In addition to the regular operation and maintenance costs of the pond itself, there will be further costs for the treatment of arsenic. These will amount to P4 million per year for each of the fifteen producing wells.

There are no scientific studies of the interactive effects of boron and arsenic on a rice field; hence there is no basis at this point for determining whether or not the effects on productivity will be less severe if the arsenic is removed. There may also be some residual effects on the aquatic ecosystems, but these are not identifiable.

Capital costs for a water-purification system are estimated at P25 million and annual operating and maintenance costs at P7.5 million.

(4) Discharge of Untreated Effluent into the Bao River. A thermal pond will cost P7 million. A pipeline some six or seven kilometers long would take two years to build at a cost of P13 million. Operation and maintenance costs will be P6.2 million a year.

Since the point of discharge will be downstream from the diversion for irrigation, the area of the Bao River Irrigation System will not be affected by the waste fluids.

A water-purification system will be needed to serve the residents along the reaches of the Bao River below the point of discharge. Its construction will take two years at a cost of P15 million. Annual operation and maintenance costs are estimated at P4.5 million.

The information on fishery productivity used in Option (2) will be used in this option to estimate the costs to the marine environment.

(5) Discharge of Treated Effluent into the Bao River. The capital costs will be the same as in Option (4). However, the operation and maintenance costs will be higher. The annual cost of treating the waste fluids for arsenic is estimated at P4 million per producing well.

The cost of establishing a water-purification system will be lower when the fluids are treated for arsenic. The capital cost is estimated at P7.5 million, but the time needed for construction remains the same. Operation and maintenance costs of P2 million are expected.

(6)   Discharge at Sea with an Outfall at Lao Point.   This scheme will need a 22-kilometer pipeline which will take two years to build at a cost of P45 million. Its annual operating and maintenance cost will be P41.8 million.

The disposal of waste water at sea may affect the productivity of coastal fishing as well as the commercial fishing in Ormoc Bay and the Camotes Sea. Not enough information is available, however, to quantify these effects.

7.   Disposal at Sea with an Outfall at Biasong Point.   For this option a 32-kilometer pipeline would be constructed. This would take two years and would cost P65 million. Operation and maintenance costs would come to P60.8 million per year.

The productivity of marine fishing may be affected. In estimating the effects of Options (6) and (7) on marine productivity, hydrological and dispersal patterns in Ormoc Bay and the Camotes Sea should be taken into account.

ANALYSIS OF THE OPTIONS

There is enough information available to carry out an analysis of some of the major environmental effects of the various options. While the overall approach is that of cost-effectiveness analysis, individual effects are usually valued using direct productivity changes based on market prices.

The assumption is therefore made that market prices can be used to value agricultural and fishery production – that is, that there are no major distortions requiring the use of shadow prices. This may or may not be correct for the Philippines, but in this example no price adjustments are made. A similar assumption is made in the case of imported capital equipment used in the disposal systems and for petroleum products used to power the pumps and other equipment involved. Again, if major distortions like subsidies, foreign exchange controls, or capital rationing exist, then shadow prices would be needed.

The present value of the direct costs and the associated environmental costs for each of the proposed waste-water disposal schemes are calculated with a discount rate of 15 percent and an estimated project life for the geothermal power plant of thirty years. Table A.10 presents the calculations of direct capital, OM and R costs for Options (1), (2), (3) and (6). Table A.11 presents the calculation of environmental resource costs for the same options.

The results of these calculations for all seven options are summarized in Table A.12. Without including the values of environmental costs, Option (4), in which untreated waste fluids are discharged into the Bao River, would have been chosen

Table A.10: Calculation of Direct Capital, OM and R Costs of Alternative Waste-water Disposal Options (in Pesos)

Option (1)	Reinjection	Million P

1. Construction (2 years)
   a. reinjection wells 70
   b. pipeline 20
   c. stand-by system 17

    107

   construction cost per year = 107/2

    = 53.50

2. Operation and maintenance per year 10.4
   Cash flow:

year	1	2	3	...	30
million P	53.5	53.5	10.4		10.4

   Present value at 15 percent discount rate

   year 1 = 53.5 × 0.8696 = 46.5
   year 2 = 53.5 × 0.7561 = 40.4
   years 3–30 = 10.4 × 4.9405 = 51.4

   Present value of total
    direct cost 138.30

Option (2)	Discharge to Mahiao River without Treatment	Million P

1. Construction
   a. thermal pond (1 year) 7
   b. water supply system (2 years) 50

2. Operation and maintenance per year
   a. thermal pond 0.0433
   b. water supply system 15.0
   Cash flow:

year	1	2	3	...	30
million P	25	25	15		15.0
		7	0.0433		0.0433
cost/year	25	32	15.0433		15.0433

   Present value at 15 percent discount rate
   year 1 = 25 × 0.8696 = 21.74
   year 2 = 32 × 0.7561 = 24.20
   years 3–30 = 15.0433 × 4.9405 = 74.32

   Present value of total
    direct cost 120.26

Option (3)	*Discharge to Mahiao River with Treatment*

1. Construction   *Million P*
   a. thermal pond (1 year)   7
   b. water supply system (2 years)   25

2. Operation and maintenance per year
   a. thermal pond   0.0433
   b. arsenic removal for 15 steam-
      producing wells (at 4 million
      each)   60
   c. water supply system   7.5

Cash flow:

year	1	2	3	...	30
million P	12.5	12.5	0.0433		0.0433
		7	60		60
			7.5		7.5
cost/year	12.5	19.5	67.5433		67.5433

Present value at 15 percent discount rate

           10.87   14.74   (——333.7——)

Present value of total direct cost   = 10.87
                                        14.74
                                      333.7
                                      359.3

Option (6)	*Disposal at Sea with an Outfall at Lao Point*

1. Construction   *Million P*
   a. pipeline (2 years)   45

2. Operation and maintenance per year   41.8

Cash flow:

year	1	2	3	...	30
million P	22.5	22.5	41.8		41.8

Present					
value	19.57	17.01	(——206.51——)		

Present value of total direct cost   = 243.09

106

Table A.11: Calculation of Environmental and Resource Costs of Alternative Waste-water Disposal Options (in Pesos)

Option (1)   Reinjection

The environmental cost cannot be estimated, although it involves: (i) possible loss of potential energy; (ii) treatment cost for dissolved solids in reinjection pipes; and (iii) additional environmental problems from chemicals used to keep the reinjection pipe from being clogged.

Option (2)   Discharge to Mahiao River without Treatment

The environmental effects in this case include both the quantifiable and the non-quantifiable consequences, namely:

1. rice productivity: 4,000 ha per season serviced by BRIS;
2. river fishery: no data;
3. stock health;
4. laundry, bathing and human health; and
5. sea ecosystems.

Quantifiable Effects:
Value of rice production loss:
Total rice area = 4,000 ha
Return/ha for irrigated rice
    (average 1975–8) = 1,838 – 1,492 = P346
    Return/ha for non-irrigated rice = 1,082 – 758 = P324
    Annual loss if irrigation water cannot be used due to heavy contamination

$$= 4,000 \times 346 \times 2 - [4,000 \times 324]$$
$$= 2,768,000 - 1,296,000$$
$$= \text{P1.47 million}$$

Present value of rice loss at 15 percent discount rate (years 3–30)
1.47 × 4.9405   = P7.26 million
Value of fishery product loss:
Assuming total loss of product currently obtained

From data on average costs and return profile of fishing operation in Leyte, the net return

$$= 6,914 - 4,918$$
$$= 1,996$$
or $$= 29 \text{ percent of gross return}$$

Total value of fishery product in the Camotes Sea and Ormoc Bay in 1980
                         = P39.4 million
Annual loss of fishery product   = 39.4 × 0.29 gross return
                         = P11.4 million

Present value of fishery loss at 15 percent discount rate (years 3–30)
11.4 × 4.9405   = P56.3 million

Non-quantifiable Effects:
River fishery, stock health, human health, loss of water use for laundry and bathing, effects on the marine ecosystems, plus possible family dislocation.

Option (3)	*Discharge to Mahiao River with Treatment*

Environmental Effects:
1. rice productivity: unknown;
2. river fishery: no data;
3. stock health, laundry, bathing and human health: non-quantifiable but less than Alternative 2; and
4. marine ecosystems: unknown.

Option (6)	*Disposal at Sea*

Environmental Effects: unknown effects on marine ecosystems.

Table A.12: Costs of Waste Disposal under Alternative Schemes (in million Pesos)

Alternative	*Direct Cost*	*Environ- ment Cost*	*Total Measured Costs*	*Non-quantifiable or Non-Measured Costs*
1. Reinjection	138.3	Unknown	138.3	Energy loss
2. Untreated Mahiao Discharge	120.2	Rice 7.3 Fishery 56.5	184.0	Freshwater fishery, stock health, laundry, bathing uses, human health, sea ecosystems
3. Treated Mahiao Discharge	359.3		359.3	Rice production and a lower loss on items in Alternative 2 with the exception of sea ecosystems
4. Untreated Bao Discharge	81.1	Fishery 56.5	137.6	Freshwater fishery, stock health, domestic use, human health, sea ecosystems
5. Treated Bao Discharge	359.1		359.1	Less than Alternative 4
6. Lao Point	243.1	Unknown	243.1	Non-quantifiable but high
7. Biasong Point	353.2	Unknown	353.2	Non-quantifiable but high

Source: Dixon and Hufschmidt (eds) (1986).

because it entailed the lowest direct cost. Once the environmental effects are valued and added to the direct cost, the total direct and indirect measurable costs are obtained.

Options (3), (5), (6) and (7) can be rejected because they are all relatively costly compared to Options (1), (2) and (4), among which the choice would now seem to lie.

If the decision is based strictly on measurable costs, then Option (4) is the cheapest scheme. However, both Options (4) and (2) may seriously contaminate the marine ecosystem with unknown and unquantifiable results. Option (2), which calls for the discharge of untreated waste into the Mahiao River, is rejected because not only does it pollute, like Option (4), but it is also more expensive. In contrast, the main non-quantifiable effect of Option (1) is the possible loss of energy from the lowering of the steam temperature. Hence reinjection becomes the most desirable method, although its total measured costs are slightly higher than for Option (4). In this case a slightly larger measured cost in Option (1) is preferred over the greater environmental uncertainty inherent in Option (4), the least-cost alternative.

Case Study 3: Thailand Fisheries Development

This case study is an *ex-post* analysis of a fisheries development project funded by the Asian Development Bank. It emphasizes the importance of a broad economic analysis of development projects and the need to take into account other effects that may result from "misuse" or the redirection of the capital facilities provided by projects. It is difficult to use fixed capital investments (for example dams, power stations or roads) for anything other than their intended purpose, but mobile resources like boats, vehicles or airplanes may be redirected to alternative uses. For example, two-wheeled tractors may be provided for agriculture but are actually used as transport vehicles by being hooked to small wagons. Or, again, subsidized fertilizer provided for one crop may be used on another crop which is not part of the project.

The Thai fishery project is just such a case. It was approved as both economically sound and socially desirable, but the capital for the project was redirected with consequent economic losses and depletion of resources. It may have been difficult, if not impossible, to have prevented this diversion, but a broader analysis could have identified this possibility and, in appraising the project, taken it into consideration.

BACKGROUND

In 1970 the government of Thailand approached the Asian Development Bank for a loan to finance a trawler project in order to develop further its demersal fishery. The Bank refused to lend the funds because it felt that Thailand's demersal fishing was fully exploited and that any additional capacity would lead to overfishing. In 1974 the government again asked for a loan, this time to develop its pelagic fishery, a resource that was not fully exploited. At the end of 1975 the Bank approved a loan to buy 135 gill-netting and purse-seining vessels and five fishery-related, land-based cold stores. By 1978, however, approximately 70 percent of the project vessels had been converted into trawlers (which were profitable to operate on a private basis) and were being used to catch already overfished demersal stocks.

Fish is the principal source of animal protein in the Thai diet and is a major source of foreign exchange earnings. In 1977 Thailand's total fish production was 2.2 million metric tons (mt). It declined to 1.8 million in 1980 but recovered to over 2.2 million in 1983. The present contribution from inland fisheries is minimal and the marine catch makes up over 90 percent of the total. These production data must be interpreted with caution, however, because a significant proportion of the landings are caught outside Thai waters.

With the establishment of exclusive economic zones (EEZs) in the early 1970s, Thai fishermen lost the legal right to fish in large parts of their traditional fishing grounds. These have become parts of the EEZs of other countries like Vietnam, Kampuchea and Burma. The attempt to maintain the high levels of catch has put intense pressure on the remaining Thai EEZ in the Gulf of Thailand and the Andaman Sea and has forced Thai trawlers to wander into the EEZs of other nations. It is estimated that 29 percent of the 1983 catch was taken outside Thai waters.

The official catch statistics, which include extraterritorial catches, give the misleading impression that a high volume of catch is being maintained. However, research vessel findings indicate that demersal stocks in the Gulf of Thailand have been reduced by approximately 88 percent. As access to other waters becomes more restricted, Thai boats will increasingly be forced to fish within their own EEZ; this will undoubtedly exacerbate the overfishing problem.

Even though the gross volume of catch has been maintained, the quality of the fishery has deteriorated. The volume of the demersal catch of food fish has declined by over 30 percent since the early 1970s, while the volume of trash fish (part of which is processed into fishmeal) has increased by over 20 percent. The net result is a decrease in fish suitable either for direct human consumption or for export and an increase in trash fish products.

ANALYSIS

It was anticipated that the pelagic fishery project would produce considerable socioeconomic benefits in the form of increased income to fishermen, increased employment in the project area and increased availability of fish for domestic consumption, especially in the low-income areas of the North and Northeast regions of Thailand where *per capita* fish consumption is low.

Although the individual owners of the vessels provided by the project probably benefited from it, there may be no positive net economic benefits since the project catch cannot be considered to be incremental. No precautions were taken to guard against the refitting of the vessels as trawlers; these boats were then used to fish the demersal stock in direct competition with the artisanal fishermen who have no alternative employment and are among the poorest members of Thai society. The consequence has been an increase in underemployment and unemployment in already depressed coastal areas.

110

The increased pressure in the demersal fishery has also contributed to its decline. Since the early 1970s the demersal catch in both the Gulf of Thailand and the Andaman Sea has been decreasing at the same time as the number of vessels fishing the region have increased. Tables A.13 and A.14 show that the maximum sustainable yield (MSY) could be taken with far fewer vessels – the catch per hour and per vessel has decreased steadily over time. As a consequence there has been a significant increase in production costs because current fishing practices, involving too many vessels, result in the inefficient use of fuel, labor and capital resources.

At the same time, overfishing has led to a change in the composition of the catches from large, high-value fish to smaller and less valuable fish. The result, of course, has been a decline in the value of the catch, a narrowing of profit margins and reduced income for the fishermen.

Although marine landings have increased over the last decade, *per capita* fish consumption has declined at a rate approximately equal to population growth (see

Table A.13: Catch, Standardized Fishing Effort and Catch Rate in the Gulf of Thailand Trawl Fishery

Year	Effort ('000 trawl hours)	Demersal Catch ('000 mt)	Catch Rate (kg/hr)
1960	–	50.85	–
1961	358	106.55	297.6
1962	515	102.70	199.4
1963	672	198.20	294.9
1964	1,114	320.60	287.8
1965	1,471	343.10	233.2
1966	2,051	363.80	177.4
1967	2,773	437.42	157.7
1968	3,493	513.38	147.0
1969	3,621	518.65	143.2
1970	3,876	530,89	137.0
1971	6,065	608.58	100.3
1972	7,362	711.295	96.6
1973	5,810	828.149	142.7
1974	6,439	600.263	93.2
1975	9,683	746.238	77.1
1976	8,185	757.332	92.5
1977	11,216	841.288	75.0
1978	9,978	810.757	81.3
1979	9,932	791.490	79.7
1980	12,610	781.675	62.0
1981	15,672	780.000	49.8

Source: Asian Development Bank, *Thailand Fisheries Sector Study* (Manila, 1985), Table 25.

Table A.14: Changes in Catch and Fishing Effort on the Andaman Sea Trawl
Fishery

Year	Demersal Fish (mt)	Number of Trawlers
1970	183,060	251
1971	177,089	270
1972	168,457	372
1973	203,599	553
1974	198,315	479
1975	170,360	421
1976	211,500	371
1977	159,892	456
1978	147,811	673
1979	150,355	817
1980	137,707	1077
1981	140,367	?

Source: Asian Development Bank, *Thailand Fisheries Sector Study* (Manila, 1985), Table 27.

Table A.15). This is due to the increase in the catch of trash fish and to expanding exports. The MSY for Thailand's national waters is estimated at only 1.46 million mt (Table A.16), considerably less than the actual catches from these waters; this has exacerbated the depletion of resources. As access to extraterritorial waters is increasingly denied to Thai fishermen, the situation will probably deteriorate.

It is obvious from the qualitative analysis that the project has not met its stated objectives. Accurate data on the changes in the composition and value of the catch and on the losses to artisanal fishermen were not readily available, so a full case study cannot be presented here. However, appropriate data are probably available in Thailand and a more complete analysis using them would clearly demonstrate the problems inherent in the project. The technique that should have been used to examine the effects of this project is the basic change-in-productivity approach outlined in Chapter 4.

At one level the initial appraisal was correct in examining the benefits and costs as outlined in the project documents. The shortcoming of the initial analysis lay in its failure to consider what would happen if capital stock were redirected. Had this been taken into account, certain loan covenants could have been secured or measures taken to guarantee that the fishing boats should be used only for their original purpose. The economic analysis could easily have pointed out the costs of overexploiting the resources which would result from redirecting the use of the boats.

112

Table A.15: Apparent Consumption of Fish, 1970–83 ('000 mt)

	Fish Production				Trade		Apparent Consumption	
Year	Marine Landings	(+) Freshwater Landings	(−) Food Fish Used for Fishmeal	(−) Trash[a]	(+) Imports	(−) Exports[b]	Total	kg/ capita
1970	1,336	113	–	487	14	55	921	25.7
1971	1,470	117	6	655	16	50	892	24.2
1972	1,548	131	2	719	15	77	896	23.4
1973	1,538	141	7	804	19	120	767	19.4
1974	1,351	159	12	690	20	111	717	17.4
1975	1,394	161	13	635	17	104	820	19.3
1976	1,552	147	21	621	25	128	954	22.1
1977	2,067	122	43	836	18	164	1,164	26.3
1978	1,958	141	58	847	29	211	1,012	22.4
1979	1,813	133	24	784	79	239	978	21.1
1980	1,648	144	26	787	43	232	790	16.8
1981	1,824	165	29	797	47	292	918	19.3
1982	1,987	134	26	813	46	398	930	19.2
1983	2,100	150[c]	40[d]	841[c]	80[d]	390[c]	1,059	21.5
Average	1,685	140	22	737	33	184	915	21.3

[a] Excludes small quantities (up to 15,000 mt) of shellfish used as fertilizer or for fishmeal.
[b] Adjusted to whole fish equivalent basis.
[c] Preliminary.
[d] Estimate.
Source: Asian Development Bank, *Thailand Fisheries Sector Study* (Manila, 1985), Table 23.

Table A.16: Estimated MSY for Thailand's National Waters ('000 mt)

Gulf of Thailand	
Demersal	845
Pelagic	365
Andaman Sea	
Demersal	180
Pelagic	71
Total	1,461

Source: Asian Development Bank, *Thailand Fisheries Sector Study* (Manila, 1985), Table 28.

Case Study 4: Gohor Lama Palm Oil Processing Plant

In 1975 a loan of $11.3 million was advanced to Indonesia by the Asian Development Bank for the construction of a palm oil processing plant at Gohor Lama in Northern Sumatra. In 1983 the project was evaluated by the Post-Evaluation Office and was generally found to be very successful. It was completed on time and came in under budget. Designed as an integral part of an ongoing program of oil palm development, the plant consisted of processing facilities and the related infrastructure for the extraction and export of crude oil.

Given the nature of the project (processing a highly perishable commodity with considerable value added), the economic internal rate of return is high. In the post-evaluation report it was estimated to be 32 percent. The report did note that "process efficiency and pollution control measures require strengthening". This case study briefly examines the pollution problems of the project.

THE ORIGINAL PROJECT

In the original appraisal of the project, made in 1975, it was stated that "water supply would be drawn from the Wampu River and wastes disposed of through clarification ponds and a canal into the Basilam River. The use of clarification ponds would eliminate any pollution problem in the foreseeable future." The cost estimates for the project included $80,000 for "pollution control".

The *ex-post* project evaluation, however, noted that pollution of the river is occurring as only limited anaerobic or aerobic digestion is taking place before the effluent is discharged. Having a high biological oxygen demand (BOD), the effluent affects the water quality of the river. Whereas palm oil mill effluent has a natural BOD of 20,000mg/l, a target BOD level of less than 500mg/l has been mentioned in Indonesia. In Malaysia the government has set stringent standards for effluents; a BOD limit of not more than 100mg/1 has been established for new mills.

High levels of BOD harm aquatic life by removing most of the available oxygen, thereby killing the fish. In addition, the high organic content of the effluent serves as a fertilizer for aquatic weeds and other plant forms. The decomposition of these adversely affects the smell and taste of the water and renders it unfit for drinking for both people and animals. The effects of the effluent beyond the site were not considered in either the initial project appraisal or in the subsequent project evaluation. These could have been evaluated by means of the change-in-productivity and replacement-cost approaches outlined in Chapter 5. Had this been done, the following environmental effects may have been examined:

(i) Fish in the Basilam River killed by high BOD loading (analyzed by the productivity approach).

(ii) Other animal or plant life directly affected by the change in the quality of the water. For example, the effects on crops grown on land irrigated by water from the river (analyzed by the productivity approach).

114

(iii) Contamination of the water supplies used both by people and by animals and the costs incurred in replacing the water from other sources (analyzed by the replacement-cost approach).

(iv) Additional water-treatment measures needed by downstream users (analyzed by the mitigation-cost approach).

Without knowing more about where the people downstream from the project live and who they are, we can only make hypotheses about the nature and extent of the effluent's effects on the environment. These effects could, however, be measured and valued, largely by use of market-based techniques. Although the initial project appraisal called for pollution control, the measures that were actually taken were only partially successful. If a fuller analysis of the environmental costs of disposing of effluent had been carried out in 1975, greater attention and greater resources could have been devoted to environmental protection. The project itself has been successful and it would seem that the additional costs of BOD treatment would not significantly have lowered either the economic or financial rates of return – the EIRR or the FIRR. To install the means of controlling pollution now will be more expensive than if it had been done when the plant was built.

Case study 5: Soil Erosion and Degradation in the Northern Thai Uplands

This case study, based on a longer version prepared by Pitsanu Attaviroj[1] and found in Dixon, James and Sherman, eds (forthcoming), examines the economic dimensions of current and proposed land-use practices in upland rain-fed agricultural areas in northern Thailand. The study area has been occupied and used for upland cultivation over two decades and now suffers from land degradation. The study is concerned with the effects of land degradation, especially soil erosion, and examines both on-site and off-site effects. The main study site of 1,300 rai (208 ha) is representative of the average situation in the northern upland region. Within that area, the study focuses on a site of 7 rai (1.12 ha) which is the size of the average farm (1 rai = 0.16 hectare).

Three alternative land-management systems are examined and compared: exploitive monocropping, land development alone, and conservation farming. The results of the analysis show exploitive monocropping to be an undesirable practice and conservation farming systems to generate the highest net benefits. The study also highlights the importance of the rate of adoption of new cultivation techniques by

[1] The author acknowledges assistance provided by the Kingdom of Thailand Ministry of Agriculture and Cooperatives, Department of Land Development, and National Environment Board, and Officers and Staff of the Thai–Australia–World Bank Land Development Project, especially Mr W.F. Buddee.

farmers and calls for the rapid introduction of conservation farming systems in all upland areas of northern Thailand.

BACKGROUND

Management of the uplands of northern Thailand is largely exploitive. Weed control is usually less than ideal and levels of production are generally low. Few farmers practice relay cropping and rotation of legumes with cereals; the majority grow only one crop per year.

The major limitation to production on these soils is poor management. In order to develop cropping systems that will be viable in the long term, it is necessary to find not only technical solutions and to ensure that techniques are appropriate, but also to develop social and economic conditions to encourage their adoption in practice.

This case study reports the results of a land-development and research project conducted by the Department of Land Development, with support from the Australian government and the World Bank. The project is part of the Northern Agriculture Development Project and is known as the Thai–Australia–World Bank Land Development (TAWLD) Project.

PHYSICAL ENVIRONMENT

The study area is shown in Figure A.2. Topography divides the northern region of Thailand into two sub-regions, the Upper and Lower North. The three major land forms are lowlands, uplands and highlands. The lowlands are generally fertile alluvial areas of flat to gently undulating terrain. The uplands comprise older alluvial deposits that occur as a series of terraces to about 500 meters above sea level. The highlands range in altitude from 500 to 2,500 meters above sea level and from elevated flat plateaus to mountains with steep-sided valleys.

The soils in the region vary with the topography and most upland soils have low fertility. Available soil-moisture capacity of most upland soils of northern Thailand is low and constitutes a major constraint to crop production. Ninety percent or more of the annual rainfall occurs during the wet season. The average annual rainfall is about 1,200mm but there are wide variations within the region.

Soil erosion is a serious problem. According to official surveys, about 28 percent of the total area of the Northern Region is suffering from erosion, mostly severe or very severe. When the area of flat land is subtracted, the proportion of land at risk is clearly much higher.

ON-SITE AND OFF-SITE ENVIRONMENTAL IMPACTS

Increasingly intensive cultivation of the uplands using traditional practices and exploitive cropping systems is leading to serious erosion and the degradation of soil fertility. The most significant of the changes *on-site* is the depletion of organic

FIGURE A.2: *Study Area of the TAWLD Project in Northern Thailand*

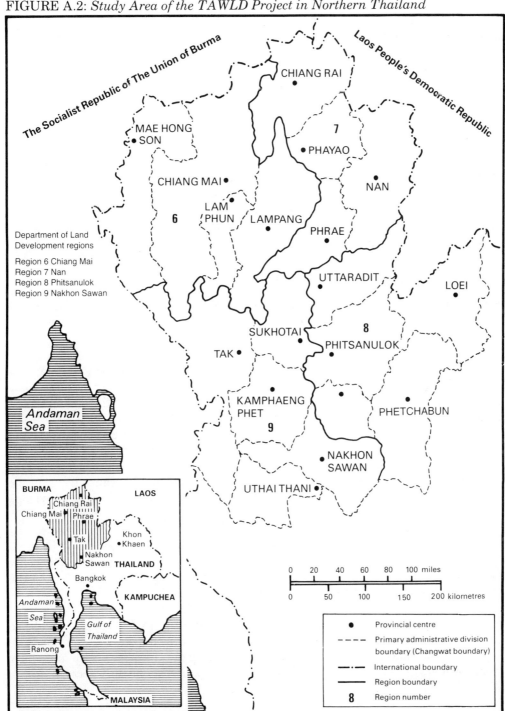

Source: Dixon, James, Sherman (eds) (forthcoming).

matter and the decreased availability of phosphorus, nitrogen, potassium and important trace elements. Field experiments also indicate an increase in soil-bulk density and a decrease in infiltration rates with clearing and cultivation of land.

The composite effect of all these changes has been a decline in production potential. Experience indicates that this is not uniform but varies with both soil type and crops grown. The decline in yield over time has been more pronounced in rice than in corn. Differences in the rates of decline in fertility for rice and corn, and the inability of fertilizer to correct rice-yield declines, probably reflect the greater dependence of rice on higher organic-matter levels and good soil structure.

Serious *off-site* effects have also occurred, including a loss of forestry resources and siltation of downstream water supplies. Forestry losses have resulted from timber poaching, an increase in farm area, and reinstatement of farm land previously abandoned to bush fallow. Siltation downstream has led to lower levels of water in reservoirs, depletion of hydroelectric capacity, degradation of the drainage system and consequent flooding as far away as Bangkok. There has also been a reduction in river depth, impeding shipping and necessitating dredging operations.

LAND-DEVELOPMENT ALTERNATIVES

Several different approaches to land management have been tried. Each approach requires different inputs and produces different levels of crop yields and environmental effects.

Exploitive monocropping. For more than two decades the increasing demand for land has been accommodated by expansion into the uplands. In general, the farmers have occupied and utilized areas of forest and secondary regrowth to supplement income from lowland farms. The exploitive practices adopted generally involve the burning of organic residues in the dry season, followed by mechanical or hand cultivation and sowing of the crop. Inputs of both time and materials are low. This alternative is considered the most likely to be adopted by the average farmer, left to his own devices. There is little incentive to conserve the land because the average farmer usually lacks one or more of the following: land tenure, technical knowledge and access to credit markets.

If exploitive monocropping continues it can be expected to result in decreasing production and increasing problems from soil erosion and consequent siltation. Some land is already so severely degraded that its rehabilitation would be a long and expensive task. However, most of the land is at the stage where the effects of the erosion and degradation that has occurred to date could be ameliorated.

Reversion to long-term swidden agriculture. Swidden (slash and burn) agriculture can provide a low-cost stable alternative but it requires that land-use pressure be substantially reduced. As this would mean relocating or otherwise employing many of the farmers, it is probably not politically, socially or economically acceptable.

Land development alone. There are two components in the decline of production potential – soil erosion and land degradation. On-site land degradation in most circumstances is by far the more serious. The control or prevention of soil erosion alone does not solve the problem. Land development alone (that is, construction of physical soil-conservation measures) seeks only to control the erosion. In all other respects, it is the same as exploitive monoculture. In the short term, however, most of the yield decline is attributable to degradation of the soil, which is not affected by these measures. Further, such works are relatively expensive and depend on World Bank credit to maintain a significant program. When the current credit is no longer available, the government's capacity to undertake this activity will be significantly diminished.

Conservation farming. Conservation farming systems include measures such as contour ploughing, contour sowing, strip cropping and the use of mulch to control erosion. They also involve green manure, cover cropping and intercropping practices which contribute to erosion control and also maintain soil organic-matter levels, improving and maintaining fertility at adequate levels. Provided the soils have not been unreasonably degraded, recovery of the land after treatment is rapid. This applies to most areas in the North.

Various cropping systems are suitable. They can be based on rice or corn, or both in combination. The rotation must include a legume phase or phases that generate sufficient organic matter to ensure that the level of soil organic matter is maintained (approximately 10 tons/ha/annum). Generally, farmers plant approximately one-third of their land to rice and two-thirds to other crops.

ECONOMIC ANALYSIS

Three main land-use alternatives are evaluated in the economic analysis:
- to allow exploitive monocropping, with its consequent continued erosion and degradation;
- to construct physical works aimed at minimizing soil erosion alone; and
- to control erosion and degradation through conservation farming practices, either alone or in combination with physical works.

The planning horizon is fifteen years. Discount rates of 5, 10, and 20 percent are used to translate future benefits and costs into present values. The sensitivity of the results to different adoption rates of the new strategies by the farmers is also tested. Adoption rates of 5, 10, and 15 percent per annum are used. Net present values are calculated for each management option, under different discount rates and adoption rates.

The study presents a comprehensive analysis of both on-site and off-site effects. Effects on both crop productivity and the environment are evaluated. Valuations of identified on-site benefits and costs are based on market prices and documented field data. Off-site benefits are measured as a reduction in off-site costs compared to the level of off-site costs that would occur with the continuation of exploitive mono-cropping. As such, this is an example of with-and-without-project analysis using costs avoided (off-site environmental costs) as a measure of potential benefits.

ON-SITE BENEFITS AND COSTS

On-site costs are the costs of production, and on-site benefits are the value of crops. For the alternatives involving land development, capital and maintenance costs are included.

For all alternatives, on-site benefits are based on average crop prices during the 1980–83 period:

Crop	*Price* (approximately 25 baht = US$ 1)
Rice	2.90 baht/kg
Maize	2.26 baht/kg
Mung bean	6.36 baht/kg
Peanut	6.56 baht/kg

Exploitive monocropping. It is estimated that newly cleared forest land will yield 300–400 kg/rai of rice, with declining yields through time. The rate of decline is estimated by the equation:

$$Y = 2{,}689 - 492.8X + 41.34X^2 - .147X^3$$

where Y is the rice yield in kg/ha and X is the number of years.

This assumes initial yields of 358 kg/rai, declining to 120 kg/rai in year 9. Farmers will grow monoculture rice until yields decline to 120 kg/rai, at which point farming becomes unprofitable. The analysis assumes half of the land is left fallow each year and that on reaching the lower yield, land is fallowed for five years. For corn, the decline in yields is slower than for rice and differs according to whether the farmer has good or average soils. Equations for the time trends are:

Average soils (tons/ha) : $Y = 2.7 - 1.75 \log(X)$
Good Soils (tons/ha) : $Y = 2.938 - 0.021X$

The yields on average soils are assumed to commence at 432 kg/rai and reach 214 kg/rai in six years. It is estimated that 25 percent of the area farmed has good soils, the remainder having average soils. On-site costs for exploitive monocropping are low, as the only requirements are land preparation, seed and labor.

Land development alone. As previously explained, this strategy seeks to control only soil erosion, not soil degradation. In the estimation of on-site benefits, it is

120

assumed that farmers continue to exploit the land if assisted with land development, regardless of tenure or utilization practices. Yield declines are thus assumed to be the same as for exploitive monoculture. However, intensity of land use increases. It is assumed that farmers use all of the land annually. The provision of access tracks is considered a benefit to landholders, but this benefit has not been quantified.

The main on-site costs are associated with initial capital works and ongoing land maintenance. Farming costs are minimal, as with exploitive monoculture.

Capital works include land selection, farm development and access tracks. The Thai government developed 124,368 rai up to 1985. The average cost of this work was 1,255 baht/rai.

In addition to capital costs, land development requires maintenance of access tracks and conservation banks. Project experience has shown that .021km per rai of bank and .006km per rai of track are necessary. Maintenance costs are 4,623 baht per kilometer of bank and 4,495 baht per kilometer of access tracks. Total maintenance costs per year are thus 124 baht/rai.

Conservation farming. Conservation farming practices can be undertaken with or without conservation works used in the land-development option. Both situations are evaluated. The rate at which farmers can be persuaded to adopt such practices is important. To test the sensitivity of this, the analysis considers the situation where 5 percent of farmers adopt in the first year and 5 percent of the balance in each following year; similarly, the analysis was reported for 10 and 15 percent adoption rates.

As regards on-site benefits, both research and on-farm demonstrations have produced rapid yield responses to the adoption of conservation farming systems.

Yields are as follows:

Crops	Year 1 (kg/rai)	Year 2 onwards (kg/rai)
Corn	400	450
Mung bean	120	140
Peanut	250	250
Black bean	green manure only	
Rice	300	400

Conservation farming requires greater direct farm inputs than exploitive mono-cropping, and the associated costs are included in the analysis. Where conservation works are also adopted, the works and capital costs are the same as for the land-development option. Maintenance costs are also the same as for the land-development option.

OFF-SITE BENEFITS AND COSTS

The off-site benefits of land development and conservation farming consist of reduced off-site damage costs compared with exploitive monocropping. To calculate the benefits, off-site damage costs must be estimated for all the alternatives. The methods used to derive the estimates are presented below. The major costs are associated with forest encroachment and siltation downstream of the project area.

Exploitive monocropping. During 1975–82 forest encroachment occurred in northern Thailand at the rate of 1.4 million rai/year. While some of this is due to timber poaching, 450 000 rai/year were used as additional farm area. For the purpose of the study, it was assumed that 0.2 million rai/year of forest were used to replace degraded lands. The annual cost in lost timber production from the area is estimated to be 330 million baht/year. It has been assumed that this loss would continue at the same rate every year.

Sedimentation is measured by suspended loads. Total sediment loads of the northern Thai rivers are comparable to rivers and similar catchments around the world. The effect on the four major dams and sixteen smaller reservoirs has been a depletion in storage capacity estimated at 18.18 million m^3/year.

Assuming a necessary annual water allocation of 2,500 m^3/rai of land cropped, the annual storage depletion from the total sediment inflow represents a loss of 7,272 rai of irrigable land per annum ($18.18 \times 10^6/2,500$). The income lost from an irrigated rice crop was estimated at 552 baht/rai for a total of 4.01 million baht each year, which will accumulate over time.

A similar argument applies to the depletion of hydroelectric capacity. If the capacity of the dam to provide water for this purpose depreciates in proportion to sedimentation rate, then the annual loss would be 1.706 million KWh. At a value of 1.50 baht per kWh, this involves a loss of 2.559 million baht/year. This cost would accumulate annually, eventually totaling 38.385 million baht in year 15.

Sedimentation and consequent degradation of the Chao Phraya River is also taking place. Nineteen million m^3 of sediment are dredged from the first 18 kilometers of the river every year, at a cost of 424 million baht, to keep the channel open to shipping. The additional cost of relieving the flood situation in Bangkok has not been included in the analysis because of the complexity of evaluating all effects.

Land development alone. A reduction in all off-site costs is assumed, consistent with the reduction in soil erosion attributable to land development. The universal soil-loss equation is used to evaluate soil-loss potential. Erosion rates are reduced by 29–39 percent through soil-conservation works. A mean reduction of 34 percent is used in the analysis; consequently erosion-related costs of this option are approximately two-thirds of the costs in the exploitive monocropping case.

Forest encroachment will still occur under this option, so there is no saving in this respect. Soil degradation will continue, and it is assumed that land will be allowed to revert to bush fallow when production falls to an unacceptable level.

Conservation farming. Off-site costs are reduced to reflect the reductions in soil erosion and forest encroachment brought about by the change in land use. The adoption of conservation farming practices will reduce erosion, and hence erosion-related damages, by 67 percent. With the inclusion of contour banks at normal spacing, the reduction in soil erosion is 76–79 percent. A rate of 78 percent is used in the analysis.

As agricultural stability is attained under conservation farming it is assumed that there will be no further forest encroachment, therefore avoiding the costs due to encroachment that occur under the other two options. This will happen whether conservation farming is used alone, or in conjunction with land development.

RESULTS

Only a summary of the results of the economic analysis can be presented here. Full details appear in Attaviroj (1986).

EVALUATION OF ALTERNATIVES

Time streams of net benefits for all the alternatives are shown in Table A.17. The effect of the discount rate on the present value of net benefits is described in Table A.18. The calculations indicate that exploitive monocropping produces positive net benefits for five years and negative net benefits thereafter. Whether this system is economically viable depends on the discount rate. High discount rates put more weight on quick returns; hence the high returns in years 1 to 5 may outweigh the negative returns in the future.

The negative returns to land development relate largely to the capital costs incurred in year 1. The positive values of years 2 to 5 cannot outweigh this initial cost or the negative returns expected from year 6 onwards.

Conservation farming systems provide high net present values at all discount rates. It is unlikely, however, that such systems would ever be adopted without land development because steep land would require some conservation works. Despite the initial costs of necessary works, conservation farming systems with land development still produce high net benefits, although at higher discount rates the impact of capital costs and low on-site benefits in early years has a significant effect on NPV.

EFFECTS OF ADOPTION RATE

Table A.19 shows the NPV for a fifteen-year period at various adoption rates of conservation farming systems. The results in Tables A.17 and A.18 assumed

Table A.17: Net Benefits from Land-Use Alternatives in Northern Upland Region (million baht)

Year	Exploitive Monocrop	Land Development Alone	Conservation Farming Alone	Conservation Farming plus Land Development
1	3,367	−5,394	2,851	−8,272
2	2,374	4,151	4,790	4,838
3	1,608	2,975	4,788	4,836
4	948	2,014	4,785	4,835
5	357	86	4,783	3,730
6	−184	463	4,781	4,832
7	−1,042	−895	4,779	4,831
8	−1,427	−1,308	4,777	4,829
9	−1,800	−1,695	4,775	4,828
10	−2,096	−3,033	4,772	3,723
11	−2,451	−2,282	4,770	4,825
12	−1,129	705	4,768	4,823
13	−1,956	−585	4,766	4,822
14	−2,587	−1,487	4,764	4,820
15	−2,549	−2,145	4,761	3,715

Table A.18: NPV of Farming Strategies over Fifteen Years for the Northern Region of Thailand (million baht)

Discount Rates	Exploitive Monocropping	Land Development Alone	Farming Systems	
			− Land Dev't	+ Land Dev't
5%	−2,114	−4,244	47,757	35,582
10%	1,147	−2,155	34,599	23,458
20%	3,608	−640	20,749	10,981

Note: Assumes that 8.9 million rai of upland are cropped.

Table A.19: NPV over Fifteen Years at Farming Systems Adoption Rates of 5 percent, 10 percent, 15 percent per year (million baht)

Discount Rates	Adoption Rates		
	5%	10%	15%
5%	11,196	14,735	21,868
10%	9,562	11,969	16,595
15%	7,427	8,688	10,921

Source: Dixon, James and Sherman (eds) (forthcoming).

immediate adoption of the new technique. These results indicate substantial rewards following high rates of adoption and would appear to justify substantial expenditure on education and advisory programs that encourage farmers to use conservation farming methods.

POLICY IMPLICATIONS

On the basis of the economic analysis conducted for this case study, conservation farming systems should be introduced in all areas of upland agriculture in northern Thailand as quickly as possible. Exploitive monoculture and burning should be discouraged.

Land development should not be undertaken unless accompanied by the introduction of conservation farming systems. Even then, where initial rates of adoption of farming systems are expected to be slow, only the minimum work necessary to reduce the erosion hazard to acceptable levels should be undertaken. Works should not be constructed on lands with slopes of less than 5 percent; on steeper land, works should be constructed only as necessary in particular cases.

Priority should be given to the promotion of farming systems in those areas currently being intensively farmed where degradation is occurring and the erosion risk is high. More generally, it is considered that concern for soil degradation and erosion should be given a higher priority in the national program. The promotion of conservation cropping systems and farming practices should be carried out on several fronts.

Comprehensive, well-orchestrated awareness programs should be conducted through the schools and the media. A special promotional effort should be initiated through the Ministry of Agriculture and Cooperatives, Department of Agricultural Extension's Training and Visit System aimed at increasing the adoption rate of conservation systems and practices.

These initiatives may need to be supported by legislation or regulations that require farmers in particularly hazardous situations either to adopt some minimum conservation procedures or at least to cease using the most hazardous practices.

References

Arrow, K.J. and R.C. Lind (1970) "Uncertainty and the Evaluation of Public Investment Decisions". *American Economic Review* 60, pp. 364–78.

Asian Development Bank (1975) *Appraisal of the Fisheries Development Project in Thailand*. Manila: Asian Development Bank.

—— (1983) *Appraisal of the Hill Forest Development Project in the Kingdom of Nepal*. Manila: Asian Development Bank.

—— (1984) *Project Performance Audit Report on Fisheries Development Project in the Kingdom of Thailand*. Manila: Asian Development Bank.

—— (1986) *Environmental Planning and Management*. Manila: Asian Development Bank.

—— (1987) *Environmental Planning and Management and the Project Cycle*. ADB Environment Paper No. 1. Manila: Asian Development Bank.

Attaviroj, P. (1986) *Soil Erosion and Degradation, Northern Thai Uplands: An Economic Study*. Paper presented to the International Conference on the Economics of Dryland Degradation and Rehabilitation, 10–14 March 1986. Canberra, Australia.

Baumol, W.J. (1968) "On the Social Rate of Discount". *American Economic Review* 58, pp. 788–802.

Carpenter, R.A. (ed.) (1983) *Natural Systems for Development: What Planners Need to Know*. New York: Macmillan.

Ciriacy-Wantrup, S.V. (1968) *Resource Conservation* (2nd edn). Berkeley: University of California Press.

Clawson, M. (1959) *Methods of Measuring Demand for and Value of Outdoor Recreation*. RFF Reprint No. 10. Washington, DC: Resources for the Future.

Clawson, M. and J.L. Knetsch (1966) *Economics of Outdoor Recreation*. Baltimore: Johns Hopkins University Press for Resources for the Future.

Conrad, J. (1980) "Quasi-Option Value and the Expected Value of Information". *Quarterly Journal of Economics* 92, pp. 813–19.

Cummings, R., D. Brookshire and W. Schulze (1986) *Valuing Environmental Goods: A State of the Art Assessment of the Contingent Valuation Method*. Totowa, NJ: Rowan & Allenheld.

Dixon, J.A. and M.M. Hufschmidt (eds) (1986) *Economic Valuation Techniques for the Environment: A Case Study Workbook*. Baltimore: Johns Hopkins University Press.

Dixon, J.A., D.E. James and P.B. Sherman (eds) (forthcoming) *Economics of Dryland Management: Case Study Reader*.

Fleming, W.M. (1983) "Phewa Tal Catchment Management Program: Benefits and Costs of Forestry and Soil Conservation in Nepal", in L.S. Hamilton (ed.) *Forest and Watershed Development and Conservation in Asia and the Pacific*. Boulder, CO.: Westview Press.

Freeman, A.M. III (1979) *The Benefits of Environmental Improvement: Theory and Practice*. Baltimore: Johns Hopkins University Press.

Gittinger, J.P. (1982) *Economic Analysis of Agricultural Projects*. Baltimore: Johns Hopkins University Press.

Graham, D.A. (1981) "Cost-Benefit Analysis Under Uncertainty". *American Economic Review* 71, pp. 715–25.

Haimes, Y.Y. (ed.) (1981) *Risk Benefit Analysis in Water Resources Planning and Management*. New York: Plenum Press.

Harrison, D. Jr and D.L. Rubinfeld (1978a) "Hedonic Housing Prices and the Demand for Clean Air". *Journal of Environmental Economics and Management* 5, pp. 81–102.

―――― (1978b) "The Distribution of Benefits from Improvements in Urban Air Quality". *Journal of Environmental Economics and Management* 5, pp. 313–32.

Haveman, R. (1969) "The Opportunity Cost of Displaced Private Spending and the Social Discount Rate". *Water Resources Research* 5, pp. 947–57.

Helmers, F.L.C.H. (1979) *Project Planning and Income Distribution*. The Hague: Martinus Nijhoff.

Henry, C. (1974) "Option Values in the Economics of Irreplaceable Assets". *Review of Economic Studies*, Symposium on Exhaustible Resources, pp. 89–104.

Hicks, J.R. (1939) "Foundations of Welfare Economics". *Economic Journal* 49 (196).

Hufschmidt, M.M., D.E. James, A.D. Meister, B.T. Bower, and J.A. Dixon (1983) *Environment, Natural Systems and Development: An Economic Valuation Guide*. Baltimore: Johns Hopkins University Press.

Hyman, E.L. and M.M. Hufschmidt (1983) *The Relevance of Natural Resource Economics in Environmental Planning*. Working Paper. Honolulu: East–West Environment and Policy Institute.

International Union for the Conservation of Nature and Natural Resources (1980) *World Conservation Strategy*. Geneva: IUCN.

James, D.E., H.M.A. Jansen and J.B. Opschoor (1978) *Economic Approaches to Environmental Problems*. Amsterdam: Elsevier Scientific.

Jones-Lee, M.W. (1976) *The Value of Life: An Economic Analysis*. Chicago: University of Chicago Press.

Kim, S.H. and J.A. Dixon (1986) "Economic Valuation of Environmental Quality Aspects of Upland Agricultural Projects in Korea", in *Economic Valuation*

Techniques for the Environment: A Case Study Workbook, ed. J.A. Dixon and M.M. Hufschmidt. Baltimore: Johns Hopkins University Press.

Kneese, A.V. (1966) "Research Goals and Progress Towards Them", in *Environmental Quality in a Growing Economy*, ed. H. Jarrett. Baltimore: Johns Hopkins University Press.

Knetsch, J.L. and J.A. Sinden (1984) "Willingness to Pay and Compensation Demanded: Experimental Evidence of an Unexpected Disparity in Measures of Value". *Quarterly Journal of Economics* 99, pp. 507–21.

Krutilla, J.V. (1969) *On the Economics of Preservation or Development of the Lower Portion of Hell's Canyon*. Draft report to the Federal Power Commission. Washington, DC.

Krutilla, J.V. and A.C. Fisher (1985) *The Economics of Natural Environments* (revised edn). Baltimore: Johns Hopkins University Press for Resources for the Future.

Lave, L.B. and E.P. Seskin (1977) *Air Pollution and Human Health*. Baltimore: Johns Hopkins University Press for Resources for the Future.

Little, I.M.D. and J.A. Mirrlees (1974) *Project Appraisal and Planning for Developing Countries*. New York: Basic Books.

Mäler, K.G. (1977) "A Note on the Use of Property Values in Estimating Marginal Willingness to Pay for Environmental Quality". *Journal of Environmental Economics and Management* 4, pp. 355–69.

Miller, J.R. and F. Lad (1984) "Flexibility, Learning and Irreversibility in Economic Decisions: A Bayesian Approach". *Journal of Environmental Economics and Management* 11, pp. 161–72.

Mishan, E.J. (1982) *Cost-Benefit Analysis* (3rd edn). London: Allen & Unwin.

Pearce, D.W. and C.A. Nash (1981) *The Social Appraisal of Projects: A Text in Cost-Benefit Analysis*. London: Macmillan.

Pigou, A.C. (1920) *The Economics of Welfare*. London: Macmillan.

Pouliquen, C.Y. (1970) *Risk Analysis in Project Appraisal*. Baltimore: Johns Hopkins University Press.

Ray, A. (1984) *Cost-Benefit Analysis: Issues and Methodologies*. Baltimore: Johns Hopkins University Press for the World Bank.

Rees, C.P. (1983) Environmental Management in the Project Cycle. *ADB Quarterly Review* QR-4-83. Manila: Asian Development Bank.

Ridker, R.G. (1967) *Economic Costs of Air Pollution: Studies and Measurement*. New York: Praeger.

Rowe, R.D. and L.G. Chestnut (1982) *The Value of Visibility: Theory and Applications*. Cambridge MA: Abt Books.

Russell, C.S. (1973) *Residuals Management in Industry: A Case Study of Petroleum Refining*. Baltimore: Johns Hopkins University Press for Resources for the Future.

Russell, C.S. and W.J. Vaughan (1976) *Steel Production: Processes, Products, and Residuals*. Baltimore: Johns Hopkins University Press.

Squire, L. and H.G. van der Tak (1975) *Economic Analysis of Projects*. Baltimore: Johns Hopkins University Press for the World Bank.

Wilson, E.O. (ed.) (1988) *Biodiversity*. Washington, DC: National Academy Press.

Index

Page numbers in italics indicate Figures;
those in bold type refer to Tables.

acid rain, 25
aesthetic resources, 55, 84
afforestation, 87
agriculture:
    conservation, 119, 121, 123, **124**, 125;
    exploitive monocropping, 118–20,
        122–3, **124**;
    inappropriate, 6;
    slash and burn, 118–19
air pollution, 16–18, *17*, 40, 52–3, 55, 67;
    control, 16, 44
Andaman Sea demersal fishery, 110–11,
    112
Asian Development Bank (ADB), 3, 86,
    109, 114
assessment, environmental, 6–9, 16, 18;
    agriculture, 12–14;
    air pollution, 16;
    coastal zones, 14–16;
    multidisciplinary, 22;
    multipurpose dam project, 9–12;
    see also measurement; quantification
assumptions:
    on supply and demand curves, 36;
    time horizon, 38;
    in welfare economics, 19–20, 22
Attaviroj, Pitsanu, 115, 123

Balagot, Beta, 98
benefit–cost analysis (BCA), 2, 23, 35, 41,
        79;
    agriculture, 120–3;
    geothermal power plant, 98;
    hill forest project, 89, **97**;
    limitations, 77–8, 81;
    multipurpose dam project, 9
benefit/cost ration (BCR), 30–1, 34
bias, 70;
    hypothetical and strategic, 66–7;
    intergenerational, 80
bidding games, 65–7
biodiversity, 83
borrowing, cost of, 33

capital:
    opportunity cost, 32;
    redirection, 109–10
Carpenter, R.A., 7n
cash-flow analysis, extending, 29
Ciriacy-Wantrup, S.V., 83
Clawson, M., and J.L. Knetsch, 55
coastal zones development projects, 14–15;
    consequences, **15**
compensating variation, 65
consumer's surplus, 20
consumption, present v. future, 33
contingent valuation methods (CVM), 84;
    limitations, 69–71;
    techniques, 64–71

cost-analysis techniques, 58, 62–3
cost-benefit analysis, *see* benefit–cost
      analysis
cost-effectiveness:
   analysis, 23, 43–6;
   waste water disposal, 98–104, **105–8**,
      109
costless choice, 68–9
costs:
   environmental, quantification, 2–3, 5,
      37–42;
   preservation, 41–2;
   preventive, 46–9;
   relocation, 60–3;
   replacement, 59–60, 61–2;
   see also opportunity cost
cultural resources, 55, 84

dams, 9–12, 84
deforestation, 1–2, 8, 79
Delphi technique, 69
demand curves, 20, *21*, 36, 56–7;
   summation of individual, 66
development:
   coastal zones, 14–16;
   consequences, **15**;
   design, avoiding errors in, 6–7;
   human welfare basis of, 1;
   impact on incomes, 96;
   sustainable, 7n;
   see also assessment, environmental;
      costs, environmental; land
      development
discount rates, 32–4, 79–80
diseases, water-related, 14
Dixon, J.A., and M.M. Hufschmidt, 3n, 31,
      34, 91n, 98
drainage project, 48

earnings, loss of, 38–41, 49
East–West Center Environment and
      Policy Institute (EAPI), 3
ecosystem, 7n
ecosystemic linkages, 8n
Egypt, Aswan High Dam, 12, 84
energy policies, new, 8

environment, protection of, 6–7;
   see also assessment; measurement;
      quantification
equivalent variation, 65

fertilizers, 3, 11, 16
Fiji power project, 11
fish-pond construction, 38
fisheries:
   damage to, 1, 14–16;
   development, 109–12, **111–13**;
   water pollution and, 102–3
flood control, 53
foreign exchange rates, 3
forest land values, 86–92, **90, 92, 95–6**;
   with project, 92–8, **94–6**
forestry:
   development, 60, 79, 81;
   hill, 86–97;
   management, 87, 98;
   project evaluation, **97**, 98;
   yields with project, **93**
forests, overexploitation, 87
fuelwood, 91

genetic diversity, 64
geothermal power plant, 98–104, *99*,
      105–8, 109
Gittinger, J.P., 32, 34
Grandstaff, Somluckrat, 98
Guide, 2–3, 32, 36, 44, 57, 65

habitat alterations, 82
Harrison, D., and D.O. Rubinfeld, 52
Haveman, R., 33
health:
   care costs, 39–41;
   environmental changes affecting, 9
Hell's Canyon Study, 42
Henry, C., 82
Hicks, J.R., 19
historical resources, 55, 84
Hufschmidt, M.M., *et al.*, 3n
human life, value of, 83
hydroelectric power, deforestation and, 2
Hyman, E.L., and M.M. Hufschmidt, 32
hypothetical valuation, 64

income distribution, 77–8
incomes, development impact on, 96
incrementalism, 83–4
Indonesia, 48;
    palm oil processing, 38, 114–15
information bias, 70
input–output models:
    generalized, 71–2, *73*;
    limitations, 72, 74
instrument bias, 70
intergenerational equity, 79–80
internal rate of return (IRR), 31–2, 34
irreversibility, 8, 82–3
irrigation:
    deforestation affecting 2;
    mismanaged, 12–14;
    poorly designed, 6;
    water pollution and, 11, 102

Kim, S.H., and J.A. Dixon, 47–8, 59
Kirindi Oya Irrigation and Settlement
    Project, 12
Knetch, J.L., and J.A. Sinden, 70
Korea, soil stabilization, 59–60
Krutilla, J.V., and A.C. Fisher, 42, 82

land:
    development, 118–25, **124**;
    management, 115–19
land use:
    values, 89–92, **90**, **92**;
        with hill forest project, 92–8, **94–6**
    with and without forestry project,
        88–9, **90**
land values, 53–4
Latin American dam projects, 12
linear programming, 74–6

Malaysia, Kuala Lumpur quarries' dust
    fall, *17*
market prices, 23–4;
    costs valuation by, 43–9;
    in hill forest valuation, 86, 90–1;
    production change valuation by, 35–42;
    surrogate, 50–63;
    in waste water disposal analysis, 104

marketed goods as environmental
    surrogates, 58–9
measurement of impacts on environment,
    19–24;
    geothermal power plant, 98–109;
    hill forest development, 86–98;
    limitations, 77–85;
    market prices in, 23–4, 86, 90–1, 104;
        costs valuation, 43–9;
        production change valuation, 35–42,
        60;
        surrogate, 50–63;
    multidisciplinary, 30;
    palm oil processing, 114–15;
    soil erosion, 115–25;
    techniques, 24–5, **26–8**, 29–34;
        choice of, 49;
        contingent valuation, 64–71;
        generally applicable, 24, 28, 35;
        macroeconomic models, 71–6;
        potentially applicable, 24–5, 50;
    time horizon, 25, 29–30;
    see also quantification
Miller, J.R., and F. Lad, 82–3
mitigative expenditure, 46–7
monetary quantification:
    environment development costs, 5, 25,
        43, 64–76;
    see also market prices; costs
multipurpose dam project, 9–12;
    loss of economic development
        opportunities, *10*

natural resources, misuse of, 1
natural systems analysis, 12
Nepal, 38;
    hill forest, 86–97;
        land values, 86–92, **90**, **92**, 95–6;
        land values, with project, 92–8, **94–6**;
        project evaluation, **97**;
        yields with project, **93**
net present value (NPV), 30–1, 34

opportunity cost, 41–3, 49, 83;
    approach to land use value, 91–2;
    of capital, 32

option value, 82
overgrazing, 6

palm oil processing, 38, 114–15
Papua New Guinea power project, 11
pelagic fisheries development, 109–12,
    111–13
pesticides, 3, 11
Philippines:
    forestry development, 60;
    geothermal power plant, 98–104, *99*,
        105–8, 109
Pigou, A.C., 19
pollution, 72–4, *73*;
    see also air pollution; water pollution
population:
    displaced, 9, 12;
    pressure, 6
poverty, rural, 6
power:
    lines, 53–4;
    plant:
        coal-fired, 16;
        geothermal, 98–104, *99*, **105–8**, 109;
    projects, 11
preservation cost, 41–2
preventive expenditures, 46–9
production factors, 36
productivity changes, 36–8, 49, 60
project cycle, 3–5, *4*
project evaluation criteria, 30–2
property values, 51–3, *52*
public goods, 66

quantification:
    environmental changes, 8–9;
    environmental costs of development,
        2–3, 5, 37–42;
    see also measurements; monetary
        quantification
quarries' dust fall, *17*
quasi-option value, 82

recreational goods, 55–8, 64, 66, 68
regional environmental effects, 71
relocations costs, 60–3

replacement costs, 59–60, 61–2
reservoirs, sediment in, 11
return rate, internal, 31–2, 34
risk in project analyses, 80–2
road construction, 29, 38
Rowe, R.D., and L.G. Chestnut, 67
rural poverty, 6
rural–urban migration, 6

Safe Minimum Standard (SMS), 83
salinity, 8, 12
salt balance equation, *13*
sedimentation, 11, 14, 122
sensitivity analysis, 81
shadow prices, 75
shadow-project technique, 61–2
siltation, 11
social rate of time preference, 33–4
soil:
    conservation, 38, 80;
    erosion, 9, 11, 48, 59–60, 86;
        and degradation, 115–25;
    salinization, 12
species preservation, 64, 66, 69
Sri Lanka Irrigation and Settlement
        Project, 12
subsidies, 3
supply curves, 36
surrogate-market techniques, 24
survey-based valuation techniques, 65

taxation, 3
Thailand, *117*;
    fish production and consumption, **113**;
    fish-pond construction, 38;
    fisheries development, 109–12, **111–13**;
    soil erosion and degradation, 115–25,
        124
Thailand Gulf demersal fishery, 110–11,
        111
time preference, social rate of, 33–4
trade policies, 3
trade-off games, 68
travel cost, 55–8, *56*, 63

uncertainty in project analyses, 80–2
utility curves, 20, *21*

wage differentials, 54–5
waste disposal, 8–9, 40
waste water, 61;
   disposal, 98–104, **105–8**, 109
water:
   pollution, 1, 6, 14, 40, 62, 114–15;
   supply, 48, 58, 61

water-related diseases, 14
watershed management, 12
weighting, 78, 81
welfare:
   basis of development, 1;
   economics, 19–22, 37;
   environmental changes affecting,
    9
Western Samoa power project, 11
World Conservation Strategy, 7